Powerful Pedagogy
How can we teach better quicker?

In *Powerful Pedagogy*, Ruth Powley, **Love Learning Ideas** blogger and experienced teacher and school leader, debunks teaching and learning myths and shows how the more we know about pedagogy, the more able we are to make informed and efficient choices about our practice, saving ourselves valuable time. Focusing on building sequences of learning rather than one-off lessons, it is an antidote to 'quick fix' books, empowering teachers as professionals in possession of 'powerful' pedagogical knowledge that can be used to improve teaching in a sustainable way.

Powerful Pedagogy draws extensively from a wide range of educational writers and research, offering an accessible synthesis of what really works in the classroom. Together with strategies to put theories and research into practice, each chapter contains a handy list of questions for the reflective practitioner. It explores reasons for the confusion over what constitutes effective pedagogy in recent years and presents practical research-based solutions, outlining successful and efficient:

- Modelling of excellence
- Explaining for understanding
- Practising to fluency
- Questioning as assessment
- Testing to permanency
- Marking for improvement
- Planning of lessons and curriculum sequences.

Powerful Pedagogy allows teachers to understand how to make the best choices about what works in the classroom, improving the quality of teaching. It is an essential companion for trainee and experienced teachers in all sectors, and for school leaders and educational trainers.

Ruth Powley is Deputy Headteacher at Wilmslow High School, Cheshire, UK, and author of the immensely popular Love Learning Ideas blog @powley_r.

Powerful Pedagogy

Teach Better Quicker

Ruth Powley

Taylor & Francis Group

LONDON AND NEW YORK

First published 2018
by Routledge
2 Park Square, Milton Park, Abingdon, Oxon OX14 4RN

and by Routledge
711 Third Avenue, New York, NY 10017

*Routledge is an imprint of the Taylor & Francis Group,
an informa business*

© 2018 Ruth Powley

The right of Ruth Powley to be identified as author of this work has been asserted by her in accordance with sections 77 and 78 of the Copyright, Designs and Patents Act 1988.

All rights reserved. No part of this book may be reprinted or reproduced or utilised in any form or by any electronic, mechanical, or other means, now known or hereafter invented, including photocopying and recording, or in any information storage or retrieval system, without permission in writing from the publishers.

Trademark notice: Product or corporate names may be trademarks or registered trademarks, and are used only for identification and explanation without intent to infringe.

British Library Cataloguing in Publication Data
A catalogue record for this book is available from the British Library

Library of Congress Cataloging in Publication Data
A catalog record for this book has been requested

ISBN: 978-0-415-78687-4 (hbk)
ISBN: 978-0-415-78689-8 (pbk)
ISBN: 978-1-315-22661-3 (ebk)

Typeset in Sabon
by Florence Production Ltd, Stoodleigh, Devon, UK

To Richard for his support at home and
James for his support at school

Contents

	Acknowledgements	ix
	Introduction: Why don't we know what effective teaching looks like?	1
1	What is powerful pedagogy?	19
2	Four principles of effective learning	34
3	Six principles of effective instruction	49
	Planning for effective instruction Part 1: Planning effective lessons	55
4	Modelling of excellence	60
5	Explaining for understanding	77
6	Practising to fluency	95
7	Questioning as assessment	118
8	Testing to permanency	137
9	Marking for improvement	150
	Planning for effective instruction Part 2: Designing effective curriculum sequences	167
	Index	175

Acknowledgements

This book would not have come about without the inspiration provided by the educational blogging community. It was Tom Sherrington's blog on *Contemporary Educational Ideas That All Teachers Should Know About*, published in August 2014, which informed and inspired me and led to my own blog and further reading. I am very grateful to all the educational writers that I have had an opportunity to read, (and to the few that I have been fortunate enough to meet and discuss ideas with) and to all those people who have been kind enough to re-tweet or comment favourably on my blogs. This has been most appreciated.

https://teacherhead.com/2014/08/18/contemporary-educational-ideas-all-my-staff-should-know-about/

I have worked over the years with some wonderful, committed and supportive colleagues and am particularly blessed with these in my current school. This book is my 'thank you.' I hope that it helps.

Introduction
Why don't we know what effective teaching looks like?

> Pedagogy: The method and practice of teaching, especially as an academic subject or theoretical concept (Google).

The word 'pedagogy' has an interesting recent history in English education. In 1981, educational historian, Brian Simon, wrote a critique of educational practice in England, *Why No Pedagogy in England?* Using the OED definition of pedagogy as the 'science of teaching,' Simon contrasted the European concept of teaching as a 'science' to the lack of 'science' in English thinking and practice, the key feature of which he argued was its, "eclectic character, reflecting deep confusion of thought, and of aims and purposes, relating to learning and teaching – to pedagogy."[1]

Supposedly, the National Strategies (1997–2011), emerging from the national literacy and numeracy projects, were an attempt by the Department for Education and Skills (as was) to define a clear national approach to teaching, initially in primary schools, through the national literacy and numeracy strategies. *Pedagogy into Practice*, published in 2004, was intended to extend this national programme of best-practice informed professional development into secondary schools through 'pedagogically-informed' training materials, and teaching and learning frameworks covering all aspects of pedagogy:

1. Structuring learning
2. Teaching models
3. Lesson design for lower attainers
4. Lesson design for inclusion
5. Starters and plenaries
6. Modelling

7. Questioning
8. Explaining
9. Guided learning
10. Group work
11. Active engagement
12. Assessment for Learning
13. Developing reading
14. Developing writing
15. Using IT
16. Leading in learning (thinking skills)
17. Developing effective learners
18. Improving the climate for learning
19. Learning styles
20. Classroom management

The National Strategies initiative marked a renewed emphasis on the importance of effective teaching to school improvement, which was intended to create clarity around good practice. David Hargreaves and Michael Fullan believe that this "informed prescription"[2] was an attempt to curb the "era of individual classroom autonomy" which, at worst, had provided "a license to be ineffective (and not even know it)"[3] for some teachers; however, despite these well-intentioned efforts, the Sutton Trust Report *What Makes Great Teaching?* – a review into the research on effective teaching – could state with some justification in 2014, regarding understanding of effective pedagogy, that this understanding, "may not be . . . widely shared, and even where it is widely shared it may not actually be right."[4]

How did this lack of clarity over effective teaching occur?

Four reasons for confusion over what constitutes effective teaching

1. The atomisation of instruction

One reason for confusion over what constitutes effective teaching was a consequence of the atomisation of instruction by *Pedagogy into Practice* into so many disparate elements. By dividing 'pedagogy' into twenty chunks, the holistic element of instruction was underplayed. This fashion for 'listing' in education will be familiar to any teacher who has ever attempted to squeeze a series of acronyms: ICT, RWCM, VAK, and PLTS (I could go on) into their already over-filled lessons in an attempt to 'tick all the boxes' in the lesson plan.

As a consequence of *Pedagogy into Practice*, teachers, schools and professional development programmes tended to juggle between the elements of teaching, prioritising some at the expense of others.

Based on the 'this year (which always also seemed to turn into next year as well) we're focusing on starters and plenaries' approach it would have taken at least 20 years for any school to plough through the *Pedagogy into Practice* series, with the committed and well-organised school finishing in 2024.

In the prioritisation process outlined above, Assessment for Learning generally received a disproportionate amount of time, energy and professional development budget, while Explanation remained a poor relation in comparison, despite being a prerequisite for effective teaching often cited by students as a key factor in whether they regard teachers as 'good' or 'bad.' This compartmentalisation has prevented a greater focus on, and understanding of, the holistic nature of instruction, and the way in which the elements of instruction connect together. In *Making Every Lesson Count*, Shaun Allison and Andy Tharby question whether the profession has, "so over-complicated definitions of 'good practice' that it has blinded itself from some simple truths."[5]

Arguably, the effect of this atomisation has been to impede effectiveness. In *Why "What Works" Won't Work* published in 2007, Professor of Education, Gert Biesta, who has written on the purpose of education, criticised the "cookbook approach"[6] of the National Strategies and their failure to achieve their aims. Similarly, Robert Coe, Director of the largest educational research centre in a UK university – the Centre for Evaluation and Monitoring (CEM) – highlights in *Improving Education: A Triumph of Hope Over Experience* the limited impact of Assessment for Learning on educational outcomes over a period of fifteen years despite its, "near universal adoption."[7]

2. The role of Ofsted in fetishising one type of lesson

A second reason for confusion over what constitutes effective teaching was the role of Ofsted in defining effective teaching and the organisation's 'fetishisation' of a particular type of 'Ofsted' lesson. Teach First graduate and Civitas research fellow, Robert Peal, critiqued the influence of Ofsted in *Playing the Game: The Enduring Influence of the Preferred Ofsted Teaching Style*, a report published by Civitas in 2014. He found that between 2007 and 2013, Ofsted published 115 reports and resources on 'good practice,' for example *Curriculum Innovation in Schools* (2008) and *Learning: Creative Approaches that Raise Standards* (2010). According to Peal, these were marked by a preference for child-centred teaching methods and skills-based curricula. Between 2010 and 2012 in particular, Peal believes that 'independent' learning was a "precondition" of 'outstanding' teaching. Peal also found evidence that this preference continued into 2013 with only a "superficial" change in the language of written reports in 2014.[8]

According to his statistics on preferred lesson styles in 2013 secondary school inspection reports:

- 52 per cent showed a preference for 'independent' learning;
- 42 per cent showed a preference for group work;
- 18 per cent were critical of too much teacher talk; and
- 18 per cent were critical of 'passive' learning.

In Peal's sample of 130 reports he found only one report in which an inspector recommended a more teacher-led approach. Peal criticises the "'jazzy' lessons, replete with group-work, role-play and active learning" that ensued as a result of the 'Ofsted-style' approach.[9]

Robin Alexander, British academic and leader of the Cambridge Primary Review, predates this 'fetishisation' to the, "creeping hegemonisation" of the curriculum by the Literacy and Numeracy Strategies, with their 'template' of three-part lessons, interactive whole-class teaching and plenaries.[10]

Not until July 2014, did the Ofsted Handbook make it clear that, "Ofsted does not favour any particular teaching style and inspectors must not give the impression that it does."[11]

Peal believes that professional development within education has been dominated by the question "what does Ofsted want to see?"

He cites the proliferation of external training providers and popular teacher's guides, such as *The Perfect Ofsted Lesson* and *Pimp Your Lesson!*, that contributed to this culture, "de-professionalising teachers and distracting them from considering how children can best learn."[12]

In fact, the role of Ofsted during this period was a symptom rather than a cause, as demonstrated by the continued questioning endemic in schools along the lines of: 'What do Ofsted/ leadership want to see?' despite the deliberate retreat by Ofsted from defining effective teaching after 2014. Behind this question are both the assumption that there is a 'right' way to teach – an inbuilt default to the doctrinaire, and that this 'right' way is the preserve of some 'higher power', be it Ofsted, the school's leadership team or the 'expert' speaker on an inset day. Thought-provoking educational writer, and prolific blogger, David Didau[13] points out in *What if Everything You Knew About Education Was Wrong?* (a book written with the unashamed desire to "question your most deeply held assumptions about teaching and learning"[14]) the "unusual bloody-mindedness" it takes to dissent from what is "obviously right" and the guilt that a culture of forced 'active' teaching has foisted upon the profession.[15]

In their 2012 book, *Professional Capital*, arguing for a "fundamental repositioning of the future of the teaching profession,"[16] education reformers David Hargreaves and Michael Fullan believe that this "excessive prescription" has also undermined the collective capacity and responsibility that teachers have to "design and develop, inquire into, and implement good practice together." They make a comparison to Finland (a country that achieved great success in the 2006 PISA results, but whose scores have declined since) where an integral part of teachers' professionalism is their design of pedagogy and curriculum.[17]

Hargreaves and Fullan draw attention to the fact that this disorder in education is more widespread than England and predates the National Strategy. As early as 1987, educational psychologist, Lee Shulman, describing American practice, warned against the "great danger" that occurs when the principles of teaching become prescriptive and mandatory.[18]

David Hargreaves and Michael Fullan locate the growth of prescription in a wider context of the 1990s:

> In an age of globalisation, politicians were losing their grip on their own national economics and immigration policies, but they could at least promise to turn around schools by changing and controlling their captive population of teachers ... [therefore] the curriculum was standardised and sometimes even prescribed in excruciating detail.[19]

At his keynote speech to Pedagoo, London in 2013, teacher Kevin Bartle critiqued the 'fetishisation' of "Trojan Horses . . . brought into our closed network by outsiders such as governments, academics and even – dare I say it – Senior Leadership Teams."[20]

3. The lack of pedagogical underpinning in practice

> The first rule of teaching is good pedagogy. The second rule of teaching is good pedagogy. Repeat ad infinitum . . . The third rule of teaching is good pedagogy.
>
> Kevin Bartle, Bring on the Trojan Mice[21]

A third reason for confusion over what constitutes effective teaching, was a consequence of the failure (ironically given its name) to ground the National Strategies' *Pedagogy into Practice* in secure pedagogy. This failure can be placed in a broader historical context. In 1981, Brian Simon, praised in his Guardian obituary for his "life-long advocacy of equal secondary opportunities for all through comprehensive schooling"[22] decried the "vacuum" left by the historic neglect of pedagogy in England and the concomitant vulnerability to "the winds of fashion – to pedagogical initiatives which 'seemed to work.'"[23]

This lack of pedagogical underpinning exposed the National Strategies to criticism at the time.

In 2004, Robin Alexander argued strenuously in *Still No Pedagogy* that, twenty-three years after Simon had written on the subject, there was still no pedagogy in England. Alexander particularly criticised the Primary Strategy as "stylistically demeaning, conceptually weak, evidentially inadequate and culpably ignorant of recent educational history."[24]

There was a growing mismatch between the 'pedagogy' outlined in *Pedagogy into Practice*, and favoured by Ofsted, and developments in cognitive psychology.

Alexander criticised the Primary Strategy for its emphasis on individualisation, which he argued ignored the classroom research of the 1980s and international research on the limits to fully individualised teaching.[25] In 2014, in the policy paper *Why Textbooks Count*, Tim Oates, chair of the expert panel on the review of the National Curriculum (2010–13), also drew attention to the differences between English and international practice, pointing out that the education systems in Singapore, Shanghai, Japan and Finland implement a different model of student ability and progress to the English one of "individual and group differentiation."[26]

In *Brian Simon and Pedagogy* (2002), quoting Simon, Robin Alexander cites the Plowden Report of 1967 as a key influence in promoting individualisation and therefore inhibiting effective pedagogy. As Simon pointed out, if each child is regarded as being entirely individual and unique, how can general pedagogical principles be developed; therefore the individualism of the Plowden Report undermined "the very heart of the concept of pedagogy – the science of teaching." Simon's argument was that by underplaying the 'formative' power of education, such views denied its very purpose and function.[27]

In secondary schools, the apotheosis of individualisation was the publication of *Personalised Learning – a Practical Guide* in 2008 by the, now renamed, Department for Children, Schools and Families, introducing 'quality first teaching' focused on meeting all the different needs of the individuals in a class. In *What If Everything You Knew About Education Was Wrong?* David Didau explores Daniel Willingham's concept of 'meta beliefs' in education and locates this thinking as a consequence of Romantic meta-beliefs about education (that can be traced back to at least the publication of *Emile* by Rousseau in 1762.) Didau argues that this explains the "totemic power" of teaching practices such as personalisation, differentiation and independent learning.[28]

Other elements of the 'pedagogy' behind *Pedagogy into Practice* were always spurious.

The justification for learning styles in Unit 19, for example, which is based on the opinions of neuro-linguistic programming practitioners that because individuals may have a sensory preference when learning, there are three types of learner.[29]

In *Do Learners Really Know Best? Urban Legends in Education*, academics Kirschner and Merrienboer identify the following problems with 'pigeonholing' students into categories of learner:

- Most people do not fit one particular category of learning.
- There is a weak correlation between what people say about how they learn and how they actually learn; therefore a student's cognitive ability is a far better predictor of how they learn.
- At least 71 learning styles have been identified.

- Learner preference is not necessarily correlated to learning outcomes, with learners not necessarily benefiting from being taught in their 'preferred' style: "What people prefer is often not what is best for them."[30]

For these reasons, Kirschner and Merrienboer conclude:

> Though very appealing, there is no solid evidence that learning styles – as such – actually exist and that there is any benefit to adapting and designing education and instruction to these so-called styles.[31]

Paul Howard-Jones, author of the 2014 report *Education and Neuroscience: Myths and Messages*, examines the impact of 'neuromyths' about the brain on teaching in schools. He suggests that, in addition to a tendency to over-simplify:

> Wishful and anxious thinking have also been proposed as important emotional biases that contribute to the distortion of sound evidence. Low-cost and easily implemented classroom approaches can certainly cultivate wishfulness amongst educators, especially if they are fun and therefore likely to be well received by students.[32]

Similarly, in *Bad Science*, published in 2008, Ben Goldacre, whose specialism lies in unpicking the misuse of science and statistics, excoriated the

> vast empire of pseudoscience being peddled, for hard cash, in state schools up and down the country. It's called Brain Gym, it is pervasive throughout the state education system, it's swallowed whole by teachers, it's presented directly to the children they teach, and it's riddled with transparent and embarrassing nonsense.[33]

In a report by Kirschner *et al.* published in 2006 and titled, *Why Minimal Guidance During Instruction Does Not Work*, the authors are highly critical of the mismatch between discovery learning and the characteristics of working and long-term memory. In their opinion, the consequence of the fashion for such types of teaching has been that learners are expected to engage in cognitive activities that are "highly unlikely" to lead to effective learning, while teachers are forced to "pay lip service" to them.[34]

What Makes Great Pedagogy? (a 2012 publication for the National College for School Leadership) finds that, despite a "strong consensus" on the importance of effective teaching, there is little in educational literature on what constitutes this.[35] Therefore, as with 'Ofsted lessons', a lucrative commercial industry has been able to flourish around learning styles and discovery learning, leading Dr Kerry Hempenstall to suggest that, "without research as a guide, education systems are prey to all manner of gurus, publishing house promotions and ideologically-driven zealots."[36]

In their book, *What Every Teacher Needs to Know About ... Psychology*, David Didau and Nick Rose argue that we need a greater input of scientific thinking into teaching because, "without it the profession will simply continue to be vulnerable to bad ideas ... We can't rely on experience alone to keep the profession free of pseudoscientific ideas."[37]

Are teachers in England more prone to 'wishfulness' due to a lack of focus on pedagogy?

In 1981 Simon suggested in *Why No Pedagogy in England?* that in England, a pragmatic approach has led to "no concern with theory", in comparison to a continental view of pedagogy which unifies the act of teaching with the body of knowledge, argument and evidence within which it exists.[38]

This is not merely an English problem. In America, Lee Shulman also expressed frustration with the "amnesia" to be found within the teaching profession and its lack of a history of practice.[39] Similarly, in 1982, the Australians Maggs and White bemoaned the fact that, "few professionals are more steeped in mythology and less open to empirical findings than are teachers."[40]

In the absence of pedagogy or a 'history of practice,' teachers can become prey to the range of 'traps and biases' outlined in Chapter 2 of David Didau's book, *What If Everything You Knew About Education Was Wrong?* English teacher, James Theo's, blog on the subject of 'truthiness' in education in 2014 also explores this issue.[41]

As early as 2004, Alexander was criticising the primary strategy for being "deeply patronising" of teachers with its, "Ladybird language, pretty pictures ... and populist appeals to their common sense."[42]

4. The problematic nature of what good teaching 'looks' like

A final reason for the confusion over what constitutes effective teaching, is our increasing awareness that establishing what good teaching 'looks' like is problematic. Good teaching may not necessarily 'look' like anything due to the invisible nature of the learning process, which makes it hard to judge effective teaching.

In *Improving Education: A Triumph of Hope Over Experience*, Robert Coe criticises "proxies" for learning that are "easily observed but not necessarily about learning:"[43]

1. Students are busy and lots of written work is done;
2. Students are engaged, interested and motivated;
3. Students are getting attention from the teacher;
4. The classroom is orderly and calm;
5. The curriculum has been delivered; and
6. Students have been able to give correct answers.

Lee Shulman criticised the "missing paradigm" by which the quality of teaching is evaluated with insufficient reference to the quality of the subject content being taught.[44] This criticism has also been leveled at non-specialist lesson observation in schools.

In *Do We Know a Successful Teacher When We See One?* Strong *et al.* conducted experiments into whether experienced teachers and head teachers could identify 'effective' and 'ineffective' teachers based on lesson observation. Their experiments yielded an accuracy rate below the 50 per cent that would be expected by pure chance. They found that less than 1 per cent of those lessons judged to be 'inadequate' may actually have been so, and only 4 per cent of those lessons judged to be outstanding. Their findings were that 63 per cent of lesson observation judgements were wrong. It was the growing clamour against the unreliability of lesson observations that led to the abandonment of individual lesson grades in Ofsted inspections from September 2014.[45]

In *What If Everything You Knew About Education Was Wrong?* David Didau points out the 'distorting' effect of lesson observations on teaching, which he criticises as being "more interested in short-term fluff than real improvement."[46]

The move to evidence and research-based teaching

In the context outlined above, it is unsurprising that in recent years there has been a shift towards both evidence-based and research-informed teaching.

In 1996, David Hargreaves stated in the Teaching Training Agency Annual Lecture that, "teaching is not at present a research-based profession. I have no doubt that if it were, teaching would be more effective and more satisfying."[47] Writing with Michael Fullan in 2012, he locates the resurgence of the evidence-based teaching movement, by which "data drive more and more classroom decision making" in the 1990s.[48]

John Hattie's *Visible Learning*, published in 2009,[49] has been a particularly influential attempt to inform evidence-based teaching. Hattie, a proponent of evidence-based quantitative research methodologies, synthesised over 800 meta-studies spanning a 15-year period in order to draw conclusions about what works best in education. For many teachers, this was their introduction to 'effect sizes.' Similarly, the Educational Endowment Foundation (EEF),[50] established by the Sutton Trust in 2011, provides a Teaching and Learning Toolkit that offers an accessible summary of educational research, providing guidance for teachers and schools on how to best use their resources to maximise attainment.

In contrast, in 2013 researchEd[51] was founded to promote research-informed teaching, described on its website as,

> a grass-roots, teacher-led organisation aimed at improving research literacy in the educational community, dismantling myths in education, getting the best research where it is needed most, and providing a platform ... to meet and discuss what does and doesn't work in the great project of raising our children.

It was in the context outlined above of increasing criticism of the 'self-evident truths' of effective teaching promulgated during the National Strategies era that the Sutton Trust Report into *What Makes Great Teaching?* was published in 2014, its intention being to provide a starting point for an educational summit in November 2014 bringing together 80 school leaders from a range of countries to consider the latest research evidence on effective teaching.

In reaction to some of the excesses of educational faddism of the 2000s, there has also been increased interest in the work of cognitive scientists in explaining how cognitive science relates to effective teaching and learning. Examples include Daniel Willingham's book, *Why Don't Students Like School?*, published in 2009,[52] *Make it Stick* by Brown, Roediger and McDaniel, published in 2014,[53] and Robert Bjork's *Learning and Forgetting Lab*.[54]

This greater focus on evidence and research-based teaching has also permeated government policy, for example proposals by the Department for Education in its 2014–15 consultation on *A World-Class Teaching Profession* to improve the quality of teaching by using Teaching Schools to build up an evidence base of effective teaching practices.[55] Similarly, in 2015, the Carter Review of Initial Teacher Training recommended a more evidence-based approach.[56]

Evidence-based teaching in particular is not without its own perils however, as the latest manifestation of 'snake oil' greasing the wheels of education.

The fact that *Visible Learning* was described by the TES in 2008 as teaching's "Holy Grail,"[57] indicates the extent to which the search for 'silver bullets' has become entrenched in the landscape of teaching – our default to the doctrinaire and the 'higher power.' In this case the danger is that we reduce pedagogy to anything that seems likely to have a greater effect size than $d = 0.40$ which is, according to Hattie, the average effect size of a year's progress.

Back in 2004, Alexander criticised New Labour's *Education, Education, Education* project for elevating 'what works' to the status of "ultimate criterion"[58] for judging educational practice.

In contrast to Alexander's views, in *What Works Best in Education: The Politics of Collaborative Expertise*, Hattie warns teachers of the need to "demonstrate to all ... that there is a 'practice of teaching' ... and that some practices have a higher probability of being successful than others. The alternative is the demise of teacher expertise."[59]

Neither should evidence-based and research-informed teaching be seen as necessarily complementary.

Hattie actually counsels against teachers becoming researchers in their classrooms. In an article in the TES: *Leave Research to the Academics* (22 April 2015) he commented:

> I want to put the emphasis on teachers as evaluators of their impact. Be skilled at that. Whereas the whole research side, leave

that to the academics... We have got no evidence that action researchers make any difference to the quality of teaching.[60]

While Hattie believes that teachers need to exercise good cognitive decision-making skills in order to select appropriate 'interventions' he also supports the idea of licensing models to "reduce the inefficiency of rediscovery" of 'what works.' He favours support for teachers from 'evaluation experts' to judge the quality of evidence and evidence-based decision-making. This external input is apparently necessary for 'credibility.' Hattie is clear that teachers "do not have a right to... autonomy" if they are not able to teach in such a way that most of their students regularly make at least a year of progress for every year of input i.e. a 0.4 effect size or above.[61]

In *What If Everything You Knew About Education Was Wrong*, David Didau is sceptical that feedback effect sizes of 1.13 indicate that students receiving feedback make over 50 per cent more progress than those not receiving feedback. It is well worth reading Chapter 5 of Didau's book in which he cautions against the "pseudo-accuracy" of effect sizes (particularly those produced by meta-analyses) which make us believe that there are "easy solutions to difficult problems."[62]

Dylan Wiliam, doyen of thinking on assessment, has been similarly scathing, in *Leadership [for] Teacher Learning*, of effect sizes, which in some cases "strain the bounds of credulity" arguing that:

> Right now, meta-analysis is simply not a suitable technique for summarizing the relative effectiveness of different approaches to improving student learning... [teachers] would be far better advised to look at best evidence reviews of research.[63]

David Hargreaves and Michael Fullan are cautious about what they describe as:

> evidence in excess ... So-called evidence can be unclear, ambiguous, compromised, out of date, indecipherable, contested, or just plain wrong. This is not a reason to fall back on intuition or personal preferences as the sole basis for teaching. We just need to be a bit more humble and careful about what we are claiming.[64]

Similarly, in *Why "What Works" Won't Work: Evidence-Based Practice and the Democratic Deficit in Educational Research*, published in 2007, Gert Biesta, who argues against restrictive policies in education, expressed concern with the "technocratic" model being adopted by evidence-based education.

"The focus on 'what works' makes it difficult if not impossible to ask the questions of what it should work for."[65]

Biesta argued that:

- While evidence-based practice portrays professional action as an "intervention," the student and patient states are very different.
- The 'what works' agenda of evidence-based practice places too much emphasis on what is possible at the expense of what is educationally desirable.
- Research tells us 'what has worked' rather than 'what will work.'[66]

Dylan Wiliam suggests that:

> Those who want to determine what works in education are doomed to fail, because in education, "What works?" is rarely the right question, for the simple reason that in education, just about everything works somewhere, and nothing works everywhere. At the other extreme, those who want to improve their practice but think that educational research is a waste of time are likely to get nowhere because, unless they are very lucky, they will spend time improving on aspects of their practice that do not benefit their students.[67]

To conclude, a process of sedimentation has therefore occurred within teaching over the last twenty years.

Pre-National Strategies 'pedagogy' has been overlaid with National Strategies 'pedagogy,' both shot through by stratum of the influential Plowden Report. This has, in turn, been overlaid with post-National Strategies 'pedagogy' weathered by the excesses of the educational faddism of the 2000s. Phrases like 'quality first teaching' and 'assessment for learning' subsist like fossils excavated from the rock and often stranded beyond their original context and meaning, which is why the *Final report of the Commission on Assessment without Levels* published in 2015[68] resolutely avoided mention of the now loaded terminology of 'Assessment for Learning.' In the meantime, the tectonic plates of traditional versus progressive education continue to shift. The point of this geological flight of fancy is to suggest that both within and across schools our problem is no longer, 'no pedagogy' but a surfeit of 'pedagogy,' some of it not even particularly pedagogical, with teachers at various levels of the rock face depending on their last exposure to pedagogical input.

None of this is intended to denigrate what Lee Shulman describes as teachers' "wisdom of practice" [69] but it is to suggest that the knowledge base that informs teachers' choices and actions must have a secure pedagogical foundation.

Earlier in this chapter, I suggested that two assumptions operate in teaching:

- That there is a 'right' way to teach – an inbuilt default to the doctrinaire; and
- That this 'right' way is the preserve of some 'higher power.'

It is in the context of the above that this book has been given the title, *Powerful Pedagogy*.

The purpose of this book is not to provide a simplistic 'silver bullet' of 'what works,' nor to re-impose a doctrinaire model on teachers; neither is it to dwell solely in the world of theoretical discourse. This book is my own attempt to connect and combine the worlds of pedagogy and practice.

In order to be professional practitioners we need both a complex and professional understanding of pedagogy but also the ability to put this effectively into practice.

If we are to be professionals rather than technicians, we cannot be practitioners without pedagogy – a theory of practice, but equally, to be useful, that pedagogy must be directly translatable into practice. This book attempts to provide ideas for how we might achieve this.

Notes

1. Simon, B. (1981) 'Why No Pedagogy in England?' in Simon, B. and Taylor, W. (eds) *Education in the Eighties: The Central Issues*, page 124, London: Batsford
2. Barber, M. (2007) *Instruction to Deliver: Tony Blair, the Public Services and the Challenge of Delivery*, page 280, London: Methuen

3. Hargreaves, D. and Fullan, M. (2012) *Professional Capital*, page 49, Abingdon, UK: Routledge
4. Coe, R. Aloisi, C, Higgins, S. and Elliot Major, L. (2014) *What Makes Great Teaching?* page 8, The Sutton Trust
5. Allison, S. and Tharby, A. (2015) *Making Every Lesson Count*, page 2, Carmarthen, UK: Crown House
6. Biesta, G. (2007) 'Why "What Works" Won't Work: Evidence-Based Practice and the Democratic Deficit in Educational Research', *Educational Theory, Volume 57*, page 11, University of Illinois
7. Coe, R. (2013) *Improving Education: A Triumph of Hope Over Experience*, page x, Centre for Evaluation and Monitoring, Durham University
8. Peal, R. (2014) *Playing the Game: The Enduring Influence of the Preferred Ofsted Teaching Style*, pages 5 and 16, Civitas
9. Ibid. pages 5–6
10. Alexander, R. (2004) 'Still no Pedagogy? Principle, Pragmatism and Compliance in Primary Education' in *Cambridge Journal of Education, Volume 34*, page 15, Cambridge, UK: Carfax
11. Ofsted (2014) *School Inspection Handbook*, paragraph 64 of subsidiary guidance
12. Peal, R. (2014) *Playing the Game: The Enduring Influence of the Preferred Ofsted Teaching Style*, page 7, Civitas
13. www.learningspy.co.uk/archive/
14. Didau, D. (2015) *What If Everything You Knew About Education Was Wrong?* front cover sleeve, Carmarthen, UK: Crown House
15. Ibid. pages 38 and 109
16. Hargreaves, D. and Fullan, M. (2012) *Professional Capital*, page xi, Abingdon, UK: Routledge
17. Ibid. pages 49–50
18. Shulman, L. (1987) 'Knowledge and Teaching: Foundations of the New Reform' in *Harvard Educational Review, Volume 57*, page 11, Harvard College
19. Hargreaves, D. and Fullan, M. (2012) *Professional Capital*, page 37, Abingdon, UK: Routledge
20. https://dailygenius.wordpress.com/2013/02/25/bring-on-the-trojan-mice/
21. Ibid.
22. www.theguardian.com/news/2002/jan/22/guardianobituaries.highereducation
23. Alexander, R. (2002) 'Brian Simon and Pedagogy: Contribution to the Life and Work of Brian Simon', University of Leicester
24. Alexander, R. (2004) 'Still no Pedagogy? Principle, Pragmatism and Compliance in Primary Education' in *Cambridge Journal of Education, Volume 34*, page 7, Cambridge, UK: Carfax
25. Ibid. page 18
26. Oates, T. (2014) *'Why Textbooks Count'* page 12, Cambridge Assessment
27. Alexander, R. (2002) 'Brian Simon and Pedagogy: Contribution to the Life and Work of Brian Simon', University of Leicester

28. Didau, D. (2015) *What If Everything You Knew About Education Was Wrong?* page 124, Carmarthen, UK: Crown House
29. http://webarchive.nationalarchives.gov.uk/20110812234120/http://ns online.org.uk/node/97131
30. Kirschner, P. and van Merrienboer, J. (2013) 'Do Learners Really Know Best? Urban Legends in Education' in *Educational Psychologist*, Volume 48, pages 173–175, Routledge
31. Ibid. page 176
32. Howard-Jones, P. (2014) 'Neuroscience and Education: Myths and Messages' in *Nature Reviews Neuroscience*, pages 1 and 3, Macmillan
33. Goldacre, B. (2009) *Bad Science*, page 13, London: Harper Collins
34. Kirschner, P., Sweller, J. and Clark, R. (2006) 'Why Minimal Guidance During Instruction Does Not Work: An Analysis of the Failure of Constructivist, Discovery, Problem-Based, Experiential, and Inquiry-Based Teaching' in *Educational Psychologist*, Volume 41, page 76, Lawrence Erlbaum Associates
35. Husbands, C. and Pearce, J. (2012) *What Makes Great Pedagogy? Nine Claims from Research*, National College for School Leadership
36. Hempenstall, K. (2006) 'What Does Evidence-Based Practice in Education Mean?' in *Australian Journal of Learning Disabilities*, Volume 11, page 88
37. Didau, D. and Rose, N. (2016) *What Every Teacher Needs to Know About . . . Psychology*, page 209, Woodbridge, UK: John Catt
38. Simon, B. (1981) 'Why No Pedagogy in England?' in Simon, B. and Taylor, W. (eds) *Education in the Eighties: The Central Issues*, page 128, London: Batsford
39. Shulman, L. (1987) 'Knowledge and Teaching: Foundations of the New Reform' in *Harvard Educational Review*, Volume 57, page 11, Harvard College
40. Maggs, A. and White, R. (1982) 'The Educational Psychologist: Facing a New Era.' in *Psychology in the Schools*, Volume 19, page 131
41. https://othmarstrombone.wordpress.com/2014/04/14/the-truthiness-of-it-all-and-why-three-men-make-a-tiger/
42. Alexander, R. (2004) 'Still no Pedagogy? Principle, Pragmatism and Compliance in Primary Education' in *Cambridge Journal of Education*, Volume 34, page 28, Cambridge, UK: Carfax
43. Coe, R. (2013) *Improving Education: A Triumph of Hope Over Experience*, page xii, Centre for Evaluating and Monitoring, Durham University
44. Shulman, L. (1986) 'Those Who Understand: Knowledge in Teaching' in *Educational Researcher*, Volume 15, page 6, American Educational Research Association
45. Strong, M., Gargani, J., and Hacifazliog lu, O. (2011), 'Do We Know a Successful Teacher When We See One? Experiments in the identification of effective teachers' in *Journal of Teacher Education*, Volume 62, pages 367–382, SAGE
46. Didau, D. (2015) *What If Everything You Knew About Education Was Wrong?* page 292, Carmarthen, UK: Crown House

47. Hargreaves, D. (1996) *Teaching as a Research-Based Profession: Possibilities and Prospects*, page 1, The Teacher Training Agency Annual Lecture
48. Hargreaves, D. and Fullan, M. (2012) *Professional Capital*, page 47, Abingdon, UK: Routledge
49. Hattie, J. (2009) *Visible Learning*, Abingdon, UK: Routledge
50. https://educationendowmentfoundation.org.uk
51. www.workingoutwhatworks.com
52. Willingham, D. (2009) *Why Don't Students Like School?*, San Francisco, CA: Jossey-Bass
53. Brown, P., Roediger III, H., and McDaniel, M. (2014) *Make it Stick: The Science of Successful Learning*, London: Harvard University Press
54. https://bjorklab.psych.ucla.edu
55. Department for Education (2015) *A World-Class Teaching Profession*, pages 5–6
56. Department for Education (2015) *Carter Review of Initial Teacher Training*, page 8
57. www.tes.com/news/tes-archive/tes-publication/research-reveals-teachings-holy-grail
58. Alexander, R. (2004) 'Still no Pedagogy? Principle, Pragmatism and Compliance in Primary Education' in *Cambridge Journal of Education, Volume 34*, page 9, Cambridge, UK: Carfax
59. Hattie, J. (2015) *What Works Best in Education: The Politics of Collaborative Expertise*, page 2, London: Pearson
60. www.tes.com/news/school-news/breaking-news/leave-research-academics-john-hattie-tells-teachers
61. Hattie, J. (2015) *What Works Best in Education: The Politics of Collaborative Expertise*, page 18–25, London: Pearson
62. Didau, D. (2015) *What If Everything You Knew About Education Was Wrong?* page 131 and 133, Carmarthen, UK: Crown House
63. Wiliam, D. (2016) *Leadership [For] Teaching Learning: Creating a Culture Where All Teachers Improve so that All Students Succeed*, pages 97–98, West Palm Beach, FL: Learning Sciences International
64. Hargreaves, D. and Fullan, M. (2012) *Professional Capital*, page 49, Abingdon, UK: Routledge
65. Biesta, G. (2007) 'Why "What Works" Won't Work: Evidence-Based Practice and the Democratic Deficit in Educational Research', *Educational Theory, Volume 57*, page 5, University of Illinois
66. Ibid. pages 7–10 and 16
67. Wiliam, D. (2016) *Leadership [For] Teaching Learning: Creating a Culture Where All Teachers Improve so that All Students Succeed*, page 63, West Palm Beach, FL: Learning Sciences International
68. www.gov.uk/government/uploads/system/uploads/attachment_data/file/483058/Commission_on_Assessment_Without_Levels_-_report.pdf
69. Shulman, L. (1986) 'Those Who Understand: Knowledge in Teaching' in *Educational Researcher, Volume 15*, page 9, American Educational Research Association

Chapter 1

What is powerful pedagogy?

> I'm throwing everything at my students and hoping that some of it sticks.

For how many teachers would this be a relatively accurate description of their teaching practice, especially for exam classes? In the modern school, the stakes are high for students and teachers, a fact that some 'educationalists' have still failed to grasp. For many teachers and students, the description in *Preparing for a Renaissance in Assessment* by Sir Michael Barber, proponent of 'deliverology,' of "teachers and students enjoying long holidays and short hours that are out of alignment with the working days and hours of their parents and guardians"[1] would be fortunate to prompt merely a wry smile. In contradiction of Sir Michael Barber's view, a report by the Education Policy Institute into *Teacher Workload and Professional Development in England's Secondary Schools*, published in 2016, found that teachers in England were working 19 per cent longer than the OECD average, with around a fifth of teachers reporting that they worked 60 hours or more in the week surveyed.[2]

The high-cost of intervention-loaded teaching

Intervention-loaded teaching and intensive input can work when done well – as Hattie states "almost everything works,"[3] but at what cost? How many teachers and schools are adding intervention after intervention to their teaching in a Stakhanovite quest for better and better exam results, exacerbated by the current zero-sum culture of Progress 8 accountability?

This is not sustainable in the long-term for the following reasons.

1. Intervention-driven teaching is based on the premise of 'more' rather than 'better.'

This is not to say that the 'more' may not be 'better.' In an article on *Improving Teaching by Increasing 'Academic Learning Time'* Fisher *et al.* suggest that "teachers who allocate more time to a specific content area have students who achieve at higher levels than teachers who allocate less time to the same content."[4] There is much to be said for looking realistically at allocated time rather than requiring intervention 'top ups' to get through an overcrowded curriculum. However, there is a difference between a strategic programme of increasing allocated time to enhance learners' performance, and engaging in 'life-support machine' intervention to prop up inefficient teaching or inefficient learning. Given the costs in time, money and energy of intervention, it would be more efficient to take John Tomsett's advice to "just make the lessons count."[5]

In a blog written in 2014 that resonated with many teachers, Tomsett, inspirational headteacher cum blogger at Huntingdon School expressed the problem:

> Why do some students think ... that ten one hour lessons ... held after school when they and their teachers are tired, will suddenly transform them ... and make up for their lack of effort in their seven hours of lessons a fortnight over the past 18 months?

2. Intervention-driven teaching runs the risk of creating a vicious circle of inefficient pedagogy:

Teachers who are over-committed as a result of a heavy programme of interventions have no time to think about pedagogy; therefore they make inefficient pedagogical choices; therefore they have less time to think about pedagogy.

In their study into effective learning techniques, *Improving Students' Learning with Effective Learning Techniques*, Dunlosky *et al.* point out that:

> Some effective techniques are underutilized – many teachers do not learn about them, and hence many students do not use them ... Also, some learning techniques that are popular and often used by students are relatively ineffective.[6]

What is powerful pedagogy? 21

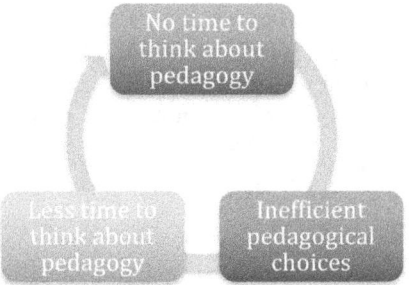

Interestingly, the report into *Teacher Workload and Professional Development in England's Secondary Schools* found that, despite working the third longest hours of the 36 countries surveyed, English teachers spent less time engaging with professional development, ranking 30th, and spending just a tenth of the time of Shanghai teachers on professional learning.[7]

3. Without a clear understanding of effective pedagogy, extra effort can be wasted.

Research sponsored by the Education Endowment Foundation into *Increasing Pupil Motivation* by using financial incentives found that:

> Even when there is a marked improvement in effort in classwork this does not translate into higher GCSE attainment ... Future studies should explore why incentives appear to change classwork effort but do not necessarily translate into higher attainment.[8]

Why did this extra classroom effort not translate into better performance?

4. Heavy workload is the main reason for teachers leaving the profession.

In *The School Leadership Journey* published in 2016, John Dunford, long-serving school leader and former national Pupil Premium Champion, suggests that retention is "a major problem to be addressed." His figures state that

25 per cent of state school teachers leave before they have spent five years in the job, with 106,000 qualified teachers under 60 never having taught in a state school. Over 40,000 teachers leave the profession each year – an annual wastage rate of around 10 per cent.[9]

Powerful Pedagogy

One solution to these problems is what I have termed 'Powerful Pedagogy.'

The more we know about pedagogy, the more able we are as teachers to make effective and efficient choices about our teaching.

This understanding of pedagogy is 'powerful' because:

- It allows us to deliver more powerful instruction.
- It empowers us as teachers to operate as professionals with a deep understanding of our practice, rather than as technicians applying the techniques of others with only a superficial grasp.
- It empowers teaching as a profession in possession of 'powerful knowledge.'

It also addresses the issues outlined in the introduction: That there is a 'right' way to teach – an inbuilt default to the doctrinaire, and that this 'right' way is the preserve of some 'higher power.'

1. It allows us to deliver more powerful instruction

Powerful Pedagogy is *not* a tick list of 'silver bullet' strategies for schools and teachers looking for quick wins – what David Didau describes in *The Secret of Literacy* as the "short-cut culture."[10] The Sutton Trust report into *What Makes Great Teaching?* explains that this over-instrumental approach is one of the two types of problem we might face when attempting to "operationalise" good pedagogy (the second is explained in the next chapter). The authors warn against attempts to over-specify, reducing pedagogy to a simplistic "checklist" of easy to observe teacher behaviours, because "the whole may be greater than the sum of its parts,"[11] in particular the important role of teacher judgement when selecting pedagogical choices.

It was the compartmentalism of instruction by *Pedagogy into Practice* into so many disparate elements that prevented a greater focus on, and understanding of, the holistic nature of instruction, and the way in which the elements of instruction connect together.

David Hargreaves and Michael Fullan warn in *Professional Capital:* "Dumb down teaching, and you will dumb down learning."[12] Similarly, in *Why "What Works" Won't Work*, Biesta argues that it is the process of thinking and deliberation which goes into pedagogical decision-making that makes "the process of choosing more intelligent."[13]

If we are to be 'experts', then we must have 'expertise'.

Rather than focusing merely on 'what works,' *Powerful Pedagogy* asks *why* 'what works' works. In *What If Everything You Knew About Education Was Wrong?* David Didau points out that teachers can "exhibit mimicry – copying what they see others doing – but without trying to develop the understanding of the expert teacher."[14] If we practice 'what works' without understanding why it works we are merely technicians, rather than professionals. As David Hargreaves and Michael Fullan point out in *Professional Capital*, their blueprint for professional teaching, "people can only teach like pros when they want and know how to do so."[15]

Knowing why 'what works' works, gives us the professional knowledge of teaching that is necessary to make informed and 'intelligent' judgements about the pedagogy available to us, and how to use this efficiently and effectively in a classroom context so that we can answer another question: *When* 'what works' works.

The role of judgement is vital, and not just that a cadre of 'super teachers' exercise sound pedagogical judgements, but that all of us do. *What Makes Great Teaching?* explains that what matters is not just the 'what' of observable teacher behaviours, but the 'why' of the judgement that goes into the choice of these behaviours.[16] 'What works' may therefore be complex and informed professional judgement rather than particular practitioner behaviours.

What Makes Great Pedagogy? published by the National College for School Leadership, finds that vital to the effectiveness of many pedagogical choices is "less their intrinsic impact than the effectiveness of the rigour with which they were pursued."[17] This suggests that implementation is as important as selection when teachers make their pedagogical choices and lends credence to Dylan Wiliam's explanation of the disappointing outcomes of Assessment for Learning (made in 2012) that, "there are very few schools where all the principles of AfL, as I understand them, are being implemented effectively."[18]

2. It empowers us as teachers to operate as professionals

In, *Still no Pedagogy? Principle, Pragmatism and Compliance in Primary Education*, Robin Alexander argues that pedagogy combines the practice of teaching with the "attendant discourse" that surrounds this; a blend of knowledge and skills, which allows teachers to make the effective pedagogical choices that constitute teaching. Alexander is therefore a critic of those who see teachers as mere technicians implementing the "educational ideas and procedures of others" rather than professionals thinking for themselves.[19] From his review of the different metaphors for teaching:

- Teaching is an art because it requires improvisation in response to contingency.
- Teaching is a craft knowledge built empirically through experience.
- Teaching is a 'science of the art of teaching' in which pedagogy is flexibly applied to respond to a particular context.

His conclusion is therefore that 'pedagogy' is a "complex enterprise" that cannot be reduced to " 'best practice' lessons downloaded from government websites."[20]

Leora Cruddas, director of policy at the Association of School and College Leaders, will have spoken for many teachers when she wrote the following in an article for the Telegraph, *Schools should decide how best to teach, not politicians*, in 2015:

> When did we decide ... that we would allow successive governments to tell us how to teach or what to teach? When did we accept that Ofsted has a mandate to prescribe our teaching practice? ... teaching is a profession, underpinned by a body of knowledge.[21]

In his book, *The School Leadership Journey*, John Dunford writes,

> Since 1988, teachers have gradually been deprofessionalised by the government's detailed centralist policies, especially on assessment, and there is no sign of any willingness on the part of the government to change this situation. Other professions, such as medicine and law, would not have stood for it, but teachers

have meekly accepted it and, in many cases, come back for more guidance and direction, such has been the lack of self-confidence in the teaching profession.[22]

Similarly, Young and Lambert, writing in *Knowledge and the Future School* suggest that teachers need, "a more confident sense of their own expertise"[23]

This re-professionalisation benefits from a collective approach. In their book, *Professional Capital*, David Hargreaves and Michael Fullan suggest that, "professional capital is something that must be acquired, spread, and reinvested by teachers themselves – individually and together. Nobody's going to be prepared to invest in anyone unless they are willing to invest in themselves."[24] In their model, "professional capital" teaching:

- "... Is technically sophisticated and difficult.
- ... Requires high levels of education and long periods of training.
- ... Is perfected through continuous improvement.
- ... Involves wise judgement informed by evidence and experience.
- ... Is a collective accomplishment and responsibility.
- ... Maximises, mediates and moderates online instruction."[25]

3. It empowers teaching as a profession in possession of 'powerful knowledge.'

Michael Young and David Lambert's book *Knowledge and the Future School* aims to be a "resource for headteachers and their staff in thinking about the curriculum."[26] They argue the case for a "Future 3" curriculum model rather than the existing models of curriculum as the delivery of either:

- A 'fixed' body of knowledge; or
- A 'socially constructed' body of knowledge with 'relevance' to the individual student.

In their 'third model' the curriculum is a tool to deliver 'powerful knowledge' rooted in "the epistemic rules of the particular [subject] specialist communities."[27] This 'powerful knowledge is defined as being:

- Distinct from 'common sense' knowledge;
- Systematic; and
- Specialised.[28]

Arguably, in recent years, teaching has been de-professionalised because 'common-sense' and 'pragmatic' pedagogy has not been seen as 'powerful knowledge' when measured against this definition.

In her controversial critique of 'early millennial' teaching, *Seven Myths about Education*, Teach First graduate and Ark Schools assessment lead, Daisy Christodolou, points out that, of the 228 lessons that she collected, which were praised by Ofsted in their publications from 2010–12, many recommended generic-skill rather than knowledge-based methods.[29]

In *Knowledge and Teaching: Foundations of the New Reform*, Lee Shulman argues against reducing teaching to "little more than personal style, artful communication, knowing some subject matter, and applying the results of recent research on teaching effectiveness"[30] In contrast, looking back to Aristotle and practice in the medieval universities, Shulman celebrates a "tradition of treating teaching as the highest demonstration of scholarship."[31]

In Shulman's view, teaching is a transformational activity involving the teacher's knowledge and judgement of "what is to be learned and how it is to be taught."[32]

Shulman's "knowledge base" for teachers is considerable:

Knowledge base for teachers

Based on Lee Shulman, *Knowledge and Teaching*,[33] and *Those Who Understand*,[34] teachers need to have knowledge of:

- Content and the structures of content knowledge;
- General pedagogy;
- Curriculum including lateral and vertical curriculum knowledge;
- Pedagogical content knowledge (more on this below);
- Learner characteristics;
- Educational contexts; and
- Educational aims.

By what right can teaching claim to be 'powerful knowledge'?

Shulman presents a compelling case for a 'powerful knowledge' base of pedagogy. In *Knowledge and the Future School*, Young and Lambert suggest that it is the very difficulty inherent in acquiring 'powerful knowledge' that,

> is why the term pedagogy, which describes the professional practice of teachers, is so important but so often undervalued. For us pedagogy refers to the theory and practice involved in taking students beyond their experience and helping them to acquire new knowledge.[35]

Use of the word 'pedagogy' makes implicit the need for theory and knowledge as well as practice in teaching.

Teaching also meets Young and Lambert's definition of 'powerful knowledge' as a systematic practice. As teachers, we generalise and think beyond particular contexts or cases, although we then need to 're-particularlise' our knowledge into our specific subject area or context. As Brian Simon argued in response to over-individualised conceptions of teaching, to achieve 'general pedagogical principles' "lies at the very heart of the concept of pedagogy – the science of teaching."[36]

Finally, teaching meets the criterion of 'powerful knowledge' because it is specialised. Young and Lambert define specialised knowledge as "developed by clearly distinguishable groups, usually occupations, with a clearly defined focus or field of enquiry and relatively fixed boundaries separating their form of expertise from other forms."[37] There is a 'tripling' of specialised knowledge within teaching:

1. The specialisation of general pedagogical knowledge outlined by Brian Simon above.
2. The particular specialisation of pedagogical content knowledge (PCK) outlined below.
3. The specialisation of the 'powerful knowledge' curriculum content taught by subject teachers.

Pedagogical Content Knowledge

Shulman introduced the definition of 'pedagogical content knowledge' in 1986 to reinforce the importance of combining content knowledge and pedagogical thinking within teaching.

Pedagogical content knowledge is the teaching (pedagogy) of subject knowledge (content). There are those who can know something very well without being able to teach it; there are also those who can teach very well without having the subject knowledge necessary to teach a particular subject well. The hackneyed joke, 'what do you teach?' to which the 'correct' answer is 'children' should really – if rather earnestly – be answered 'pedagogical content knowledge.'

Shulman defined this as "the dimension of subject knowledge for teaching ... the ways of representing and formulating the subject that make it comprehensible to others."[38] This includes an understanding of the conceptions and misconceptions related to specific subject knowledge.

The authors of the *What Makes Great Teaching?* report are clear about the importance of pedagogical content knowledge, ranking this as the first of their six components of great teaching, with strong evidence of impact on student outcomes.[39]

In *Knowledge and the Future School*, Young and Lambert argue for a curriculum of 'powerful knowledge' within schools. Without subject knowledge, we lack not just the subject knowledge itself but:

- The "shared rules of the subject [community] ... within which their questions, methods, concepts and criteria are debated and discussed."[40]
- A repertoire of subject knowledge from which to exemplify or connect information.
- Familiarity with the deep processes that underlie subject knowledge.

Young and Lambert regard powerful knowledge as that which "takes [students] ... beyond their experience"[41] precisely because it is distinct from common sense, systematic and specialised. They argue that, "the specialist character of powerful knowledge explains, at least in part, why it is experienced as difficult to acquire and why acquiring it requires specialist teachers."[42] For Young and Lambert there is also an important social dimension to powerful knowledge – implicit in the subtitle of their book (*'curriculum and social justice*'): "Adolescents . . . do not need pseudo-relevant curriculum content to reflect on their own lives . . . but knowledge that will open doors to them, to academic excellence and social justice."[43]

In *Could do Better*, Tim Oates' review of the National Curriculum, he finds that "curricular materials in high-performing nations focus on fewer topics, but also communicate the expectation that those topics will be taught in a deeper, more profound way."[44]

This focus on teaching as 'powerful knowledge' protects teachers both within and beyond schools.

As Young and Lambert point out, without subject knowledge, teachers lose power as they "rely more on their positional authority in the school and not on their specialist subject knowledge." [45]

And the importance of 'powerful knowledge' is not uncontested in the twenty-first century world even within education itself.

In *Seven Myths about Education*, described as aiming "straight for the most sacred cows,"[46] Daisy Christodolou identified seven myths about education, all associated with the transmission of knowledge, which cut at the heart of the generic skills approach fostered by programmes such as the RSA Opening Minds curriculum, with its focus on skills rather than content:

1. Facts prevent understanding.
2. Teacher-led instruction is passive.
3. The 21st century fundamentally changes everything.
4. You can always just look it up.
5. We should teach transferable skills.
6. Projects and activities are the best way to learn.
7. Teaching knowledge is indoctrination.

Young and Lambert's focus on 'powerful knowledge' also highlights the importance of pedagogy in making the curriculum 'relevant' to students: "It is teachers in their pedagogy, not curriculum designers, who draw on pupils' everyday knowledge in helping them to engage with the concepts stipulated in the curriculum and to see their relevance."[47]

Teacher educator, Michael Fordham, in his excellent blog on history teaching[48] writes:

> We have to think hard not just about *how* we teach, but also about *what* we teach. What kinds of questions do we need to ask in order to be good teachers? A large part of the answer,

I would suggest, is that we need to ask ourselves *curricular* questions.[49]

And the cost of a lack of 'Powerful Pedagogy'?

Ron Berger, based on his experiences of working in American schools, writes in *An Ethic of Excellence* that it is "painfully clear ... how many teachers have become isolated, self-protective and insecure."[50] He suggests, "it's not such a crazy idea, thinking of teachers as scholars. In fact, in prestigious American schools and in those of other countries in which teachers actually view themselves as scholars, the quality of teaching is generally superb."[51]

How have we managed to travel so far from the optimistic belief that effective teaching is transformative with a formative power to change the learning and learning capacity of young people?

And therefore it is worth us asking the questions individually and collectively as teachers:

- Do we have a sufficiently powerful understanding of effective and efficient instruction?
- Are we operating sufficiently powerfully as professionals rather than technicians?
- Are we emphasising sufficiently the powerful knowledge inherent within the teaching of pedagogical content knowledge?

Notes

1. Hill, P. and Barber, M. (2014) *Preparing for a Renaissance in Assessment*, page 12, London: Pearson
2. Sellen, P. (2016) *Teacher Workload and Professional Development in England's Secondary Schools: Insights from TALIS*, Education Policy Institute
3. Hattie, J. (2009) *Visible Learning*, page 15, Abingdon, UK: Routledge
4. Fisher, C., Marliave, R., and Filby, N., (1979) 'Improving teaching by increasing "academic learning time" in *Educational Leadership*', page 53, Belmont, CA: Fearon Pitman
5. https://johntomsett.com/2014/02/15/this-much-i-know-about-why-we-should-stop-intervening-and-focus-upon-improving-the-quality-of-teaching/
6. Dunlosky, J., Rawson, K., Marsh, E., Nathan, M., and Willingham, D. (2013) 'Improving Students' Learning with Effective Learning Techniques: Promising Directions from Cognitive and Educational Psychology' in *Psychological Sciences in the Public Interest, Volume 14(1)*, page 5, SAGE publishing
7. Sellen, P. (2016) *Teacher Workload and Professional Development in England's Secondary Schools: Insights from TALIS*, Education Policy Institute
8. Sibieta, L., Greaves, E., and Sianesi, B., (2014) *Increasing Pupil Motivation: Evaluative Report and Executive Summary*, page 2, Education Endowment Foundation
9. Dunford, J. (2016) *The School Leadership Journey*, page 129, Woodbridge, UK, John Catt
10. Didau, D. (2014) *The Secret of Literacy*, page 52, Carmarthen, UK: Crown House
11. Coe, R. Aloisi, C, Higgins, S. and Elliot Major, L. (2014) *What Makes Great Teaching?* page 10, The Sutton Trust
12. Hargreaves, D. and Fullan, M. (2012) *Professional Capital*, page xiii, Abingdon, UK: Routledge
13. Biesta, G. (2007) 'Why "What Works" Won't Work: Evidence-Based Practice and the Democratic Deficit in Educational Research', *Educational Theory, Volume 57*, page 15, University of Illinois
14. Didau, D. (2015) *What If Everything You Knew About Education Was Wrong?* page 117, Carmarthen, UK: Crown House
15. Hargreaves, D. and Fullan, M. (2012) *Professional Capital*, page 5, Abingdon, UK: Routledge
16. Coe, R. Aloisi, C, Higgins, S. and Elliot Major, L. (2014) *What Makes Great Teaching?* pages 19–20, The Sutton Trust
17. Husbands, C. and Pearce, J. (2012) *What Makes Great Pedagogy? Nine claims from research*, National College for School Leadership
18. www.tes.com/news/tes-archive/tes-publication/think-youve-implemented-assessment-learning
19. Alexander, R. (2004) 'Still no Pedagogy? Principle, Pragmatism and Compliance in Primary Education' in *Cambridge Journal of Education, Volume 34*, page 11, Cambridge, UK: Carfax

20. Ibid. page 13
21. www.telegraph.co.uk/education/educationopinion/11415058/School-should-decide-how-best-to-teach-not-politicians.html
22. Dunford, J. (2016) *The School Leadership Journey*, page 134, Woodbridge, UK: John Catt
23. Young, M. and Lambert, D. with Roberts, C. and Roberts, M. (2015) *Knowledge and the Future School*, page 4, London: Bloomsbury
24. Hargreaves, D. and Fullan, M. (2012) *Professional Capital*, pages xvi and xvii, Abingdon, UK: Routledge
25. Ibid. page 14
26. Young, M. and Lambert, D. with Roberts, C. and Roberts, M. (2015) *Knowledge and the Future School*, page 3, London: Bloomsbury
27. Ibid. page 67
28. Ibid. pages 74–75
29. Christodolou, D. (2014) *Seven Myths About Education*, London: Routledge
30. Shulman, L. (1987) 'Knowledge and Teaching: Foundations of the New Reform' in *Harvard Educational Review, Volume 57*, page 6, Harvard College
31. Shulman, L. (1986) 'Those Who Understand: Knowledge in Teaching' in *Educational Researcher, Volume 15*, page 7, American Educational Research Association
32. Shulman, L. (1987) 'Knowledge and Teaching: Foundations of the new Reform' in *Harvard Educational Review, Volume 57*, page 7, Harvard College
33. Ibid. page 8
34. Shulman, L. (1986) 'Those Who Understand: Knowledge in Teaching' in *Educational Researcher, Volume 15*, American Educational Research Association
35. Young, M. and Lambert, D. with Roberts, C. and Roberts, M. (2015) *Knowledge and the Future School*, page 19, London: Bloomsbury
36. Alexander, R. (2002) 'Brian Simon and Pedagogy: Contribution to the Life and Work of Brian Simon', University of Leicester
37. Young, M. and Lambert, D. with Roberts, C. and Roberts, M. (2015) *Knowledge and the Future School*, page 75, London: Bloomsbury
38. Shulman, L. (1986) 'Those Who Understand: Knowledge in Teaching' in *Educational Researcher, Volume 15*, page 9, American Educational Research Association
39. Coe, R. Aloisi, C, Higgins, S. and Elliot Major, L. (2014) *What Makes Great Teaching?* page 2, The Sutton Trust
40. Young, M. and Lambert, D. with Roberts, C. and Roberts, M. (2015) *Knowledge and the Future School,* pages 76–77, London: Bloomsbury
41. Ibid. page 10
42. Ibid. page 77
43. Ibid. pages 149 and 150
44. Oates, T. (2010) *Could do Better: Using International Comparisons to Refine the National Curriculum in England*, page 14, Cambridge Assessment
45. Ibid. page 103

46. www.theguardian.com/education/2014/nov/25/daisy-christodoulou-seven-myths-education-profile
47. Young, M. and Lambert, D. with Roberts, C. and Roberts, M. (2015) *Knowledge and the Future School*, page 97, London: Bloomsbury
48. https://clioetcetera.com
49. https://clioetcetera.com/2015/02/15/want-to-improve-your-teaching-study-your-subject/
50. Berger, R. (2003) *An Ethic of Excellence*, page 128, Portsmouth, NH: Heinemann
51. Ibid. pages 130–131

Chapter 2

Four principles of effective learning

Effective learning is presumably anything that causes 'learning' to become 'learned.'

Thoughts on the relationship between learning and pedagogy

In *What Makes Great Pedagogy?* Husbands and Pearce suggest that it is "impossible to develop a coherent framework for thinking about pedagogy without a conception of learning."[1] Similarly, when outlining their ten principles for effective pedagogy, James and Pollard define pedagogy as expressing, "the contingent relationship between teaching and learning."[2]

Robert Coe suggests in *Improving Education: A Triumph of Hope over Experience,* that as teachers, in order to avoid the 'proxies' for learning that we can mistake for actual learning we need to "clarify exactly what we think learning is and how it happens."[3] Similarly, the Sutton Trust Report into *What Makes Great Teaching?* outlines two dangers when trying to 'operationalise' good pedagogy:

- The danger of being too specific – outlined in Chapter 1; and
- The danger of not being specific enough.

Coe *et al.* explain that to avoid the second danger, pedagogy must be related to "something that is observable."[4]

Educational historian, Brian Simon, had a profoundly optimistic view of the transformative power of teaching on learning due to:

- Human capacity for learning; and
- The similarities in the learning process across humans.

For this reason, he argued that to emphasise individual differences was to "start from the wrong position" and that effective pedagogy must be based on "what children have in common."[5]

For all of the reasons above, this chapter therefore suggests four principles of effective learning to consider when planning teaching to ensure that this is both effective and efficient.

1. Learning happens when students think hard

The first principle is shamelessly purloined from Robert Coe and therefore even less original than when he described it as "not original" back in 2013; however Coe's question, "Where in this lesson will students have to think hard?" is indeed a useful one for teachers to ask.[6]

Make it Stick, by Brown *et al.* was written with the avowed intent of debunking fashionable ideas about the easiness of learning. Its authors point out that in fact, "learning is deeper and more durable when it's effortful."[7]

In recent years there has been a focus on making learning easier or 'fun' in order to engage students.

Many students (and teachers) do not regard thinking hard as 'fun' (unless of course they are doing it during a pub quiz or computer game!) How many teachers have entered the classroom to a chorus of, "can we do something easy today Miss?" If learning actually happens when we think hard, this trend makes effective learning less likely to occur.

David Didau highlights the potential cost of emphasising 'fun' over learning with lessons that are "more about fun than learning" and teachers experiencing "guilt and inadequacy."[8] He is also trenchant on the subject of students being able to concentrate: "If 'our kids' can't pay attention for more than five minutes then we damn well need to teach them to do so!"[9]

George Leonard suggests in *Mastery*[10] that we live in a culture at war with a proper understanding of mastery; one which lauds success, continuous progress and interest without consideration of the inevitable effort, setbacks and boredom that are part of gaining mastery. Similarly, in *Knowledge and the Future School*, Young and Lambert argue that acquiring 'powerful knowledge:'

> Always requires much dedicated effort and hard work ... It is the sense of struggle involved in acquiring knowledge that

may be at the root of the prevailing 'fear of knowledge' found among teachers.[11]

Didau and Rose explain in, *What Every Teacher Needs to Know About ... Psychology*, the difference between biological primary knowledge, which is relatively easy for humans to acquire, and culturally constructed secondary knowledge, which is not. As they point out, "there's an enormous amount of culturally specific learning required to become functionally numerate ... This kind of learning is effortful and difficult – because evolution through natural selection has not had time to shape our minds to rapidly learn this way."[12]

Thinking hard should not be confused however with making learning unsuccessful.

An American report entitled *Teaching Adolescents to Become Learners* found that students who believe that they can succeed academically:

> Are much more likely to try hard and to persevere in completing academic tasks, even if they find the work challenging or do not experience immediate success. Believing one can be successful is a prerequisite to putting forth sustained effort.[13]

Computer game designers have become highly successful at harnessing the addiction of performance improvement by combining the right blend of advancing levels of difficulty with sufficient success. David Didau points out that:

> Some kids commit many hours to playing computer games where the goal is to master the game and reach the end. They get constant and instant feedback about what works and what doesn't and then they get the opportunity to try out this feedback again and again until they get it right. Pupils who quickly throw in the towel at school are willing to persevere at *Call of Duty* until they overcome their limitations.[14]

Teachers need to find a similar blend of 'accessible challenge.'

Another challenge is the need to re-frame 'thinking hard' as a sign of success rather than failure, and an indication of effective learning. We will know that we have got there when our students greet us with the words, "can we try something really difficult today Miss?" Some teachers may be sceptical about how possible this is, but one immediate step that we can take is to lead by example in ensuring that our own attitude to thinking hard and overcoming difficulties is positive. Perhaps it is worth remembering Michael Young's *et al.* point here that, "the specialist character of powerful knowledge explains, at least in part, why it is experienced as difficult to acquire."[15] If we want the knowledge that we impart to our students to be 'powerful', then we, and they, must accept that it will be difficult to acquire, and – if we don't – then we must ask ourselves why we are spending time and resources on teaching our students 'un-powerful' knowledge.

If classroom climates are based on bribing students with easiness, conflating 'easy' with 'success' and regarding 'easy' as 'fun,' then it is not surprising that students, and teachers, shy away from difficulty.

2. *We learn what we think about*

In *Why Don't Students Like School?*, an attempt to "tell you how students' minds work, and to clarify how to use that knowledge to be a better teacher,"[16] cognitive scientist Daniel Willingham explains that memory is produced not by what we want, or try, to remember, but by "what you think about."[17]

Therefore, a key principle of an effective lesson is that the hard thinking needs to be focused on the purpose of the lesson: What is to be learned.

One problem with the 'active learning' popular in recent years has been that it can divert students' thinking away from the purpose of the lesson. The students remember creating the poster, or the game with buzzers rather than the lesson's content and underlying purpose.

A solution is to focus lesson planning on thinking hard throughout the lesson about its point.

It is impossible to tell what students are thinking about in a lesson; however, we can ensure that our lessons are structured in a way that focuses students on the purpose of the lesson, and that checks this focus throughout.

It is for this reason that formative practice and assessment within the lesson is so important:

Evidence about student achievement is elicited, interpreted and used by teachers, learners or their peers, to make decisions about the next steps in instruction that are likely to be better founded, than the decisions they would have taken in the absence of the evidence that was elicited.[18]

3. We learn when information is transferred into our long-term memory

How much do students get wrong because they don't know, and how much do they get wrong because they once knew but don't any more?

As teachers we know that there is that which our students don't know, but also that which they once knew – the all-too-familiar cry "but I got it in the lesson." There seems little point in education being a process of students continuously learning and then forgetting a sequence of information. Instead we should be giving students permanent knowledge, both propositional – knowledge 'that', and procedural – knowledge of 'how to.'

In *Make it Stick*, Brown *et al.* point out that, "to be useful, learning requires memory, so what we've learned is still there later when we need it."[19] Similarly, in *Improving Students' Learning with Effective Learning Techniques*, Dunlosky *et al.* argue that in order for students to apply learning effectively: "We unabashedly consider efforts to improve student retention of knowledge as essential."[20]

Cognitive scientist, Daniel Willingham, describes our memory as being composed of two parts:

- Working memory: The site of awareness and thinking which can hold a small amount of new information; and
- Long-term memory: A "vast storehouse"[21] of factual and procedural knowledge.

Some cognitive scientists have also postulated the existence of a 'long-term working memory,' allowing expert learners to keep the information in their long-term memory directly accessible by means of retrieval cues in their short-term memory.[22]

In part one of, *What Every Teacher Needs to Know about . . . Psychology*, David Didau, with Nick Rose – whose *Evidence Into*

Practice blog scrutinises educational research[23] – provide some extremely helpful and readable chapters on memory.[24]

The process of transfer to the long-term memory is crucial for permanent learning.

As Kirschner *et al.* point out in, *Why Minimal Guidance During Instruction Does Not Work*, "The aim of instruction is to alter long-term memory. If nothing has been changed in long-term memory, nothing has been learned."[25]

Apart from anything, this is due to the limitations of our working memories, which are capable of handling an average of only about four 'chunks' of information at any point. For this reason, in the late 1980s, cognitive scientist, John Sweller developed Cognitive Load Theory to enable teachers to design instruction that optimises students' limited working memory capacity. Incorporating this thinking into their practice allows teachers to plan for both more effective and more efficient learning.

Knowledge improves learning.

Tricot and Sweller point out that, "working memory's capacity and duration limits apply only to novel, not familiar, information."[26] This underlines the importance of prior knowledge. The 'skill' of expert problem solvers actually lies in their knowledge – the extensive experience that they are easily able to retrieve from their long-term memory.

Also crucial to learning are the creation of 'schemas' that organise knowledge. Didau and Rose point out that these "not only form the basis of long-term memory storage but also help overcome working memory limitations."[27]

Teaching is the facilitation of this process of 'learning' to 'learned.'

Effective teaching therefore needs to:

- Take into account students' lack of working memory space, and provide methods of organisation that chunk, and therefore reduce, content to be learned;
- Create schemas for students that organise their knowledge;
- Facilitate transfer of learning to students' long-term memories;
- Build up students' repository of information stored in the long-term memory; and
- Develop students' retrieval pathways allowing information to be recalled from the long-term memory.

40 Four principles of effective learning

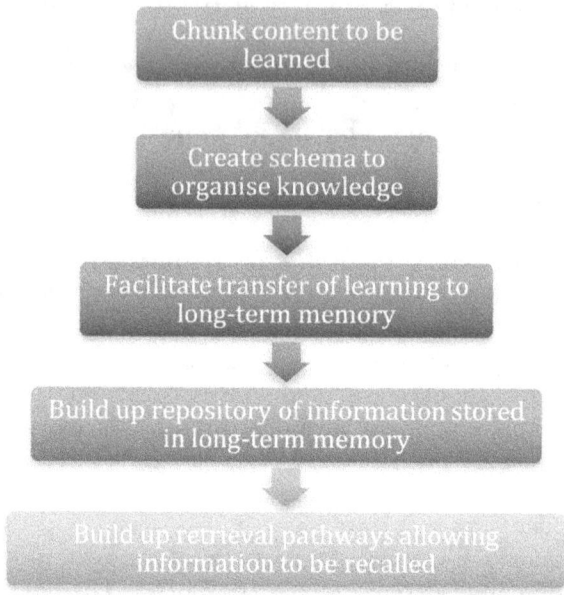

Because this process takes place over time, the best that we can hope for in any lesson is that *part* of the learning process has occurred.

Therefore, it is not necessarily helpful to see the individual lesson as the unit of learning or to believe that anything has necessarily been fully 'learned' in a lesson. David Didau highlights the absurdity of reducing this complex process of learning to "neat hour long blocks."[28]

Also, just because knowledge or expertise has been learned, does not mean that it will be retained, or effectively retrieved. Graham Nuthall, credited with the longest series of studies of teaching and learning in the classroom that has ever been carried out, suggests that "as learning occurs so does forgetting ... learning takes time and is not encapsulated in the visible here-and-now of classroom activities."[29] It is therefore vital that learning is repeated in order to embed it in the long-term memory.

There are three stages of the learning process:

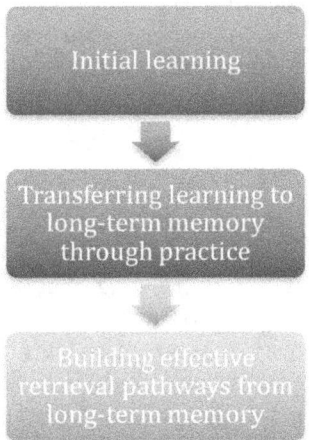

The recent focus on observable progress in individual lessons has diverted attention from both the long-term, multifaceted nature of learning, and the invisibility of the learning process. As David Didau points out in *What If Everything You Knew About Education Was Wrong?* "If teachers are judged on whether students make progress in 20 minutes, then progress will inevitably be shallow."[30]

4. Learning is counter-intuitive

As Brown *et al.* explain in *Make it Stick,* far from being 'common sense' knowledge, the most effective learning strategies can often be "counterintuitive."[31]

Similarly, researchers Meyer and Land explain that in acquiring complex understanding, some knowledge can be 'troublesome' to acquire, appearing, "alien, or counter-intuitive or even intellectually absurd at face value."[32]

Unfortunately, despite this, the increasing commercialisation of learning in recent years has exacerbated the trend towards 'truthiness' in education: The quality of seeming or being felt to be true, even if not necessarily true.

There has been a belief that the 'best' learning is easy, fun, fast and right first time, whereas in fact hard learning is stronger and more durable.

How we learn versus how we think we learn

Brown *et al.* argue that we make poor judgements about effective learning, mistaking what appears easy for what will be effective. It is in this context that 'desirable difficulties' in learning are to be understood.

'Desirable difficulties'

Robert Bjork's research at the Learning and Forgetting Lab at UCLA applies cognitive psychology in order to enhance educational practice. He finds that certain learning conditions that are difficult and appear in the short-term to impede performance actually result in greater long-term benefits than easier learning conditions. These counterintuitive learning strategies have been described as 'desirable difficulties.'

Examples of 'desirable difficulties' include:

- Varying the conditions of practice rather than keeping them constant and predictable;
- Spacing practice sessions with gaps to allow forgetting;
- Interleaving rather than blocking practice;
- Testing rather than re-studying information; and
- Reducing feedback.

Bjork also suggests that perceptual disfluency (fonts that are hard to read, or small print) can be a desirable difficulty as "the subjective difficulty of processing disfluent information can actually lead people to engage in deeper processing strategies, which then results in higher recall for those items."[33]

The 'difficult' recall of learning in the circumstances outlined above is more effective because it requires on-going 'reloading' of the knowledge to be learned from long-term memory. As permanent learning requires the 'learning' in the working memory to transfer to the 'learned' in the long-term memory, this use of long-term memory is good. This difficulty and disruption of fluency also makes the learner work harder and therefore leads to more effective learning. Bjork also suggests that it may be that different combinations of 'desirable difficulties' have "super-additive or sub-additive effects."[34]

Bjork makes a clear distinction between 'desirable difficulties' that enable the encoding, storage and retrieval process, and 'undesirable difficulties': "If the learner does not have the background knowledge or skills to respond to them successfully, they become undesirable difficulties."[35] Once again, the importance of background knowledge to effective learning is reinforced.

Common misconceptions

1. **The 'best' learners find learning easy:** Actually, "significant learning is often, or even usually, somewhat difficult;"[36] therefore easy learning should not necessarily be equated with effective learning. Didau suggests that "we can't wait until students have mastered a subject before introducing difficulty; it's the difficulty that leads to mastery."[37]

2. **The 'best' learning results in rapid progress:** In fact, "the rapid gains produced by massed practice are often evident, but the rapid forgetting that follows is not."[38] As teachers we need to focus less on rapid progress and more on secure permanency.

3. **The 'best' learning is successful:** Mistakes are important in the learning process because the making and correcting of mistakes "builds the bridges to advanced learning;"[39] therefore we must ensure that our classroom environments are not too sterile and risk averse.

4. **The 'best' learning is clear:** David Didau describes 'liminality' as a "transitional, transformative state"[40] that takes place as learners move from not knowing to knowing, or from one 'threshold' of understanding to another through grasping threshold concepts. Whilst being in a liminal state is confusing, and counter to an intuitive student and teacher desire to avoid confusion, it is also natural and necessary to the process of deepening understanding.

Threshold concepts

Meyer and Land identify 'threshold concepts' involving "troublesome knowledge" as a distinct category within the 'core concepts' that form the building blocks of understanding. They define a threshold concept as being:

> Akin to a portal, opening up a new and previously inaccessible way of thinking about something.[41]

Understanding of a threshold concept may take time to acquire, and the knowledge within it may be 'troublesome' for students to reconcile with their existing schemas; nevertheless, understanding threshold concepts is necessary in order for the learner's understanding to progress because threshold concepts are generally:

- Transformative;
- Irreversible; and
- Integrative.

The importance of threshold concepts to deep and permanent learning which moves beyond shallow knowledge and "mimicry" of understanding means that they need to feature prominently in learning and curriculum sequences, and Meyer and Land therefore suggest that they have "significant pedagogical importance."[42]

To summarise this chapter, good learning occurs when students think hard about something repeatedly over time so that it becomes embedded in long-term memory.

Good teaching is therefore getting students to do this.

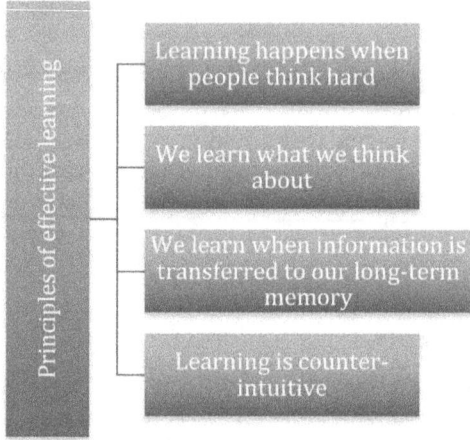

Fifteen questions for the professional practitioner to ask

Table 2.1

Question	Action
1. How do my classroom climate and lesson planning promote thinking hard, struggle and mistakes?	
2. How do my classroom climate and lesson planning promote accessible challenges and opportunities for successful learning for all students?	
3. Am I teaching 'powerful knowledge'?	
4. How do I ensure that my lesson planning enables students to think hard?	
5. How do I focus on the point and meaning of the lesson throughout the lesson so that this is what students remember?	
6. How do I chunk content so that this is more easily stored in students' long-term memory?	
7. How do I enable students to construct effective schemas of knowledge?	
8. What activities do I use to ensure that learning is transferred to students' long-term memory?	
9. How do I build students' retrieval pathways?	
10. How do I utilise 'desirable difficulties' to make students think harder?	
11. How do I plan medium-term sequences so that learning occurs across lessons rather than in individual lessons?	
12. How do I plan so that content is repeated and reinforced?	
13. How does my curriculum planning identify threshold concepts and focus on these?	
14. How do I plan 'liminal spaces' into learning to allow students to engage with, and embed understanding of these?	
15. How do I share this information with my students so that they understand the principles of learning?	

Notes

1. Husbands, C. and Pearce, J. (2012) *What Makes Great Pedagogy? Nine Claims from Research*, National College for School Leadership
2. James, M. and Pollard, A. (2011) *TLRP's Ten Principles For Effective Pedagogy: Rationale, Development, Evidence, Argument and Impact*, page 11, Faculty of Education, University of Cambridge
3. Coe, R. (2013) *Improving Education: A Triumph of Hope over Experience*, pages xii and xiii, Centre for Evaluating and Monitoring, Durham University
4. Coe, R. Aloisi, C, Higgins, S. and Elliot Major, L. (2014) *What Makes Great Teaching?* page 10, The Sutton Trust
5. Alexander, R. (2002) 'Brian Simon and Pedagogy: Contribution to the Life and Work of Brian Simon', University of Leicester
6. Coe, R. (2013) *Improving Education: A Triumph of Hope over Experience*, page xiii, Centre for Evaluating and Monitoring, Durham University
7. Brown, P., Roediger III, H., and McDaniel, M. (2014) *Make it Stick: The Science of Successful Learning*, page 3, London: Harvard University Press.
8. Didau, D. (2015) *What If Everything You Knew About Education Was Wrong?* pages 82–83, Carmarthen, UK: Crown House
9. Ibid. page 80
10. Leonard, G. (1992) *Mastery: The Keys to Success and Long-Term Fulfilment*, New York: Plume
11. Young, M. and Lambert, D. with Roberts, C. and Roberts, M. (2015) *Knowledge and the Future School*, pages 18–19, London: Bloomsbury
12. Didau, D. and Rose, N. (2016) *What Every Teacher Needs to Know about . . . Psychology*, pages 20–21, Woodbridge, UK: John Catt
13. Farrington, C., Roderick, M., Allensworth, E., Nagaoka, J., Seneca Keyes, T., Johnson, D., and Beechum, N., (2012) *Teaching Adolescents to Become Learners: The Role of Non-Cognitive Factors in Shaping School Performance, A Critical Literature Review*, page 29, Chicago, IL: University of Chicago
14. Didau, D. (2014) *The Secret of Literacy*, page 52, Carmarthen, UK: Crown House
15. Young, M. and Lambert, D. with Roberts, C. and Roberts, M. (2015) *Knowledge and the Future School*, page 77, London: Bloomsbury
16. Willingham, D. (2009) *Why Don't Students Like School?*, page 2, San Francisco, CA: Jossey-Bass
17. Ibid. page 53
18. Black, P. and Wiliam, D. (2009) 'Developing the Theory of Formative Assessment' in *Education Assessment, Evaluation and Accountability*, Volume 21, page 9
19. Brown, P., Roediger III, H., and McDaniel, M. (2014) *Make it Stick: The Science of Successful Learning*, page 2, London: Harvard University Press.
20. Dunlosky, J., Rawson, K., Marsh, E., Nathan, M., and Willingham, D. (2013) 'Improving Students' Learning with Effective Learning Techniques: Promising Directions from Cognitive and Educational

Psychology' in *Psychological Sciences in the Public Interest*, Volume 14(1), page 7, SAGE publishing
21. Willingham, D. (2009) *Why Don't Students Like School?*, page 14, San Francisco, CA: Jossey-Bass
22. Ericsson, K. and Kintsch, W. (1995) 'Long-Term Working Memory' in *Psychology Review*, Volume 102, pages 211–245
23. https://evidenceintopractice.wordpress.com
24. Didau, D. and Rose, N. (2016) *What Every Teacher Needs to Know About . . . Psychology*, Woodbridge, UK: John Catt
25. Kirschner, P., Sweller, J. and Clark, R. (2006) 'Why Minimal Guidance During Instruction Does Not Work: An Analysis of the Failure of Constructivist, Discovery, Problem-Based, Experiential, and Inquiry-Based Teaching' in *Educational Psychologist*, Volume 41, page 77, Lawrence Erlbaum Associates
26. Tricot, A. and Sweller, J. (2014) *Domain-Specific Knowledge and Why Teaching Generic Skills Does Not Work*, page 20, Toulouse
27. Didau, D. and Rose, N. (2016) *What Every Teacher Needs to Know About . . . Psychology*, page 45, Woodbridge, UK: John Catt
28. Didau, D. (2015) *What if Everything You Knew About Education was Wrong?* page 293, Carmarthen, UK: Crown House
29. Nuthall, G. (2005) 'The Cultural Myths and Realities of Classroom Teaching and Learning: A Personal Journey' in *Teachers College Record*, Volume 107, page 928
30. Didau, D. (2015) *What if Everything You Knew About Education was Wrong?* page 80–81, Carmarthen, UK: Crown House
31. Brown, P., Roediger III, H., and McDaniel, M. (2014) *Make it Stick: The Science of Successful Learning*, page 2, London: Harvard University Press.
32. Meyer, J. and Land, R. (2003) 'Threshold Concepts and Troublesome Knowledge: Linkages to Ways of Thinking and Practising Within the Disciplines' in *Improving Student Learning – Ten Years On*, C. Rust (Ed), page 2, Oxford: OCSLD
33. https://bjorklab.psych.ucla.edu/research/
34. Ibid.
35. Bjork, E. and Bjork, R. (2011) 'Making Things Hard on Yourself, but in a Good Way: Creating Desirable Difficulties to Enhance Learning' in Gernsbacher, M., Pew, R., Hough, L. and Pomerantz, J. (eds) *Psychology and the Real World: Essay Illustrating Fundamental Contibutions to Society*, page 58, New York: Worth Publications
36. Brown, P., Roediger III, H., and McDaniel, M. (2014) *Make it Stick: The Science of Successful Learning*, page 201, London: Harvard University Press
37. Didau, D. (2015) *What if Everything You Knew About Education Was Wrong?* page 271, Carmarthen, UK: Crown House
38. Brown, P., Roediger III, H., and McDaniel, M. (2014) *Make it Stick: The Science of Successful Learning*, page 47, London: Harvard University Press
39. Ibid. page 7
40. www.learningspy.co.uk/learning/learning-is-liminal-2/

41. Meyer, J. and Land, R. (2003) 'Threshold Concepts and Troublesome Knowledge: Linkages to Ways of Thinking and Practising Within the Disciplines' in *Improving Student Learning – Ten Years On*, C. Rust (Ed), page 1, Oxford: OCSLD
42. Ibid. pages 5–7 and 13

Chapter 3

Six principles of effective instruction

Effective teaching is presumably that which achieves effective learning.
The introduction to this book refers to the assumption in recent years that there is a 'right' way to teach – an inbuilt default to the doctrinaire, and that this 'right' way is the preserve of some 'higher power,' be it Ofsted, the school's leadership team or the 'expert' speaker on an inset day. Sometimes this has taken the form of mandating the structure of lessons, for example the fabled 3-part lesson. At other times, the type of teaching or activity has been prescribed or heavily recommended, for example 'activity learning' which David Didau describes in *What if Everything You Knew About Education Was Wrong?* as having been "reduced to a caricature."[1]

The premise of Powerful Pedagogy is that teachers have sufficient understanding of pedagogy to act as professionals rather than technicians, in:

- Applying pedagogy flexibly; and
- Making the many different intelligent decisions about how what is to be learned can most effectively (and efficiently) be taught.

As Lee Shulman observes in *Knowledge and Teaching*, this pedagogical decision-making process is as important to the teaching process as delivery in the classroom.[2]

It is common, and entirely desirable from the point of view of teacher morale, to compare teaching to medicine. The 2014–15 Department for Education consultation, *A World-Class Profession*, makes the welcome claim that the teaching profession should enjoy the same high status as medicine and law,[3] and it was with medicine, as another "profoundly people-centred profession,"[4] that David Hargreaves drew his comparisons in 1996 in *Teaching as a Research-Based Profession: Possibilities and Prospects.*

It is also worth remembering the optimistic belief that effective teaching is transformative with a formative power to change the learning, and learning capacity, of young people.

However, teaching is not directly comparable to brain surgery.

It is both more accessible – I would rather be taught history by a novice history teacher than have a brain tumour removed by a novice surgeon – and less accessible; it is far harder for a teacher to comment that today's lesson has been 'a complete success' because of the invisible nature of the learning process, and the fact that, with the exception of individual tuition, teaching is practised on groups rather than individuals. Instead, teaching is a challenging blend of propositional knowledge, procedural expertise and, what Shulman describes as, "wisdom of practice."[5] Like the actor, the effectiveness of the teacher's performance is also dependent on the response of their audience. Biesta argues in *Why "What Works" Won't Work* that the student/ patient analogy is not useful: "Being a student is not an illness, just as teaching is not a cure."[6]

Mindful of the two dangers outlined by the Sutton Trust Report into *What Makes Great Teaching?* when trying to "operationalise" good pedagogy:

- The danger of being too specific; and
- The danger of not being specific enough.[7]

This chapter suggests only:

- That effective learning will occur when students think hard about something repeatedly over time so that it becomes embedded, but retrievable, in long-term memory.
- That effective teaching is about facilitating this through process effective instructional choices.

There is no easy formula or set of 'magic bullets' in terms of classroom strategies;[8] neither is there supposed to be. To quote Lee Shulman in *Knowledge and Teaching*, to reduce teaching to this level would ensure that it becomes "trivialised, its complexities ignored, and its demands diminished."[9] Similarly in *Professional Capital*, David Hargreaves and Michael Fullan reject the notion that teaching is a "laundry list of simple techniques that can be prescribed and even paced so that minimally trained and modestly paid teachers can perform them satisfactorily."[10]

In the same way that effective learning occurs when students think hard about something repeatedly, effective learning about teaching occurs when teachers think hard about their teaching and pedagogical choices repeatedly.

However, it may be helpful to break down the components of teaching, not into a tick list, or twenty balls that need to be juggled and squeezed into a lesson plan, but into the logical elements of instruction.

To go back to the emphasis in *What Makes Great Teaching?* on the principles underpinning our pedagogy being "observable,"[11] this chapter therefore defines the elements of instruction as follows:

- Modelling of Excellence: That students should 'see' what they are going to think hard about and that it should be excellent.
- Explaining for Understanding: That the teacher should explain what students are going to think hard about so that they understand it.
- Practising to Fluency: That students 'think hard' about what they are learning by practising this repeatedly until their learning is fluent and transferred into long-term memory.
- Questioning as Assessment: That, given the invisible nature of learning, the teacher checks the quality of the students' learning by assessing them.
- Testing to Permanency: That the learning is tested regularly so that students can retrieve it from their long-term memory.
- Marking for Improvement: That the teacher guides students (and themselves) in the learning process by giving improving feedback.

The justification for this particular selection of elements is to imagine their absence:

- Students are not clear about what they need to learn or it is mediocre.
- Students do not understand what they need to learn.
- Students do not master what they need to learn or master it temporarily.

- The teacher does not know whether students have mastered the learning or not.
- Students forget what they have learned so it was learned for nothing.
- Students do not know how to make the improvements needed to master their learning.

However, this is by no means the only way of breaking down the elements of instruction. For example, Shaun Allison, curator of the excellent *Class Teaching* blog for Durrington High School,[12] and Andy Tharby, author of the thoughtful *Reflecting English*[13] blog, break down the principles of instruction in their book, *Making Every Lesson Count*[14] as follows:

- Challenge;
- Explanation;
- Modelling;
- Practice;
- Feedback;
- Questioning; and
- Embedding the ethos.

The elements of instruction

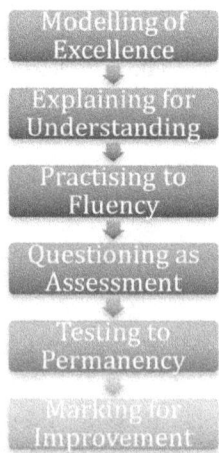

Caveat

Teaching encompasses more than the instruction process.

The elements above are *not* intended to be a definitive list of the characteristics of good teaching. If they were, this book would be much longer. Rather, they are intended to outline one approach to navigating the *instruction* process, based on the premise that quality of instruction is vital to effective teaching – *What Makes Great Teaching?* places this as its second component of great teaching with strong evidence of impact on student outcomes.[15]

In addition to this instruction process, the following are essential pre-conditions in creating a climate in which students can, and will, think hard:

- A classroom climate in which teachers build strong relationships with students, and that demands effort, cultivates curiosity and encourages risk taking and struggle – *What Makes Great Teaching?* places this as its third component of great teaching with moderate evidence of impact on student outcomes.[16]
- Efficient classroom (and behaviour) management, which promotes concentration and endeavour – *What Makes Great Teaching?* places this as its fourth component of great teaching with moderate evidence of impact on student outcomes.[17]

Notes

1. Didau, D. (2015) *What if Everything You Knew About Education Was Wrong?* page 79, Carmarthen, UK: Crown House
2. Shulman, L. (1987) 'Knowledge and Teaching: Foundations of the New Reform' in *Harvard Educational Review, Volume 57*, page 17, Harvard College
3. Department for Education (2015) *A World-Class Teaching Profession*, pages 4
4. Hargreaves, D. (1996) *Teaching as a Research-Based Profession: Possibilities and Prospects*, page 1, The Teacher Training Agency Annual Lecture
5. Shulman, L. (1986) 'Those Who Understand: Knowledge in Teaching' in *Educational Researcher, Volume 15*, page 9, American Educational Research Association
6. Biesta, G. (2007) 'Why "What Works" Won't Work: Evidence-Based Practice and the Democratic Deficit in Educational Research', *Educational Theory, Volume 57*, page 8, University of Illinois
7. Coe, R., Aloisi, C., Higgins, S. and Elliot Major, L. (2014) *What Makes Great Teaching?* page 10, The Sutton Trust

8. Muijs, R. (2010) 'Changing Classroom Practice' in D. Hargreaves, A. Lieberman, M. Fullan and D. Hopkins (eds), *Second International Handbook of Educational Change*, pages 857–868, London: Springer
9. Shulman, L. (1987) 'Knowledge and Teaching: Foundations of the New Reform' in *Harvard Educational Review*, Volume 57, page 6, Harvard College
10. Hargreaves, D. and Fullan, M. (2012) *Professional Capital*, page 25, Abingdon, UK: Routledge
11. Coe, R., Aloisi, C, Higgins, S. and Elliot Major, L. (2014) *What Makes Great Teaching?* page 10, The Sutton Trust
12. https://classteaching.wordpress.com
13. https://reflectingenglish.wordpress.com
14. Allison, S. and Tharby, A. (2015) *Making Every Lesson Count*, Carmarthen, UK: Crown House
15. Coe, R., Aloisi, C, Higgins, S. and Elliot Major, L. (2014) *What Makes Great Teaching?* page 2, The Sutton Trust
16. Ibid. page 3
17. Ibid. page 3

Planning for effective instruction Part I

Planning effective lessons

There will be a section on planning at the end of this book, but the following key points are also worth emphasising from the start:

1. An individual lesson is not the unit of learning

It is common to reduce the unit of learning to the lesson; however, Shaun Allison and Andy Tharby explain that:

> Learning is highly complex. It ebbs and flows through lessons, across schemes of work and over years. In fact, the hackneyed 'three-part' lesson of starter, main and plenary, is hopelessly simplistic. Some learning cycles are simple, quick and over in minutes. Others are much longer loops covering two, three or more lessons.[1]

Similarly, *What Makes Great Pedagogy?* suggests that "effective pedagogy is [not merely] built from a sequence of individually effective lessons."[2]

Effective learning takes place over *and between* sequences of lessons; therefore it is more appropriate to think in terms of curriculum sequences.

An undue focus on the individual lesson can both add time in the production of unnecessary lesson plans, and also detract from the planning of effective medium term curriculum sequences that map the 'learning' to 'learned' process more usefully.

In *Make it Stick* Brown *et al.* explain that, "consolidation and transition of learning to long-term storage occurs over a period of time."³ Similarly, Graham Nuthall suggests that, "Learning takes time and is not encapsulated in the visible here-and-now of classroom practices."⁴ No lesson can encapsulate the whole of the learning process from the introduction of a new concept to permanent automaticity; therefore there is no expectation that each of the six elements outlined earlier is covered in every lesson. Given what we know about how we learn effectively, learning may well take place more effectively across lessons than within them.

This is particularly the case in the teaching of 'troublesome concepts.' As David Didau explains, gaining mastery of threshold concepts is, "a messy business."⁵

2. Instructional sequences are fluid and interconnected

In the 'old days' we compartmentalised. First we planned our schemes of work in folders that lived on our shelves next to our department handbooks. Then we delivered our lessons. Then we marked our students' books retrospectively and in line with our marking policies that work be marked every week/fortnight/term/year/decade, sprinkling them with comments like "good work, keep it up" or inevitably rhetorical questions such as "where is your underlining?," *Pedagogy into Practice* inadvertently built on these compartmentalised habits by separating pedagogy into twenty stand-alone sections, as did the three-part lesson.

This 'delivery' model of education downplays the essentially 'formative' and fluid nature of teaching.

To go back to the old teaching joke: "What do you teach?" Another – again very earnest response – is "the children who are in front of me." There is a symbiotic relationship between planning, instruction and assessment. Instruction is informed by initial planning; however, the actual process of instruction, informed by assessment, results in amended planning. Teaching children is not the same as baking biscuits – a mere delivery model is insufficient, and rolling out the same power point every year ignores the importance of amending teaching to best meet the learning needs of the particular class being taught and the learning situation 'on the ground.'

In *Making Good Progress?*, Daisy Christodolou points out that Dylan Wiliam "has said that he wished he had called AfL 'responsive teaching,'"⁶ and indeed 'responsiveness' describes well the continuing and fluid teaching cycle of planning, instruction and assessment with each informing the next.

Dylan Wiliam himself describes the important "regulatory" element to responsive teaching:

> Instruction should be designed so that if the learning processes in which students are participating are not yielding the intended learning, then this becomes apparent, so that something can be done to put the learning back on track.[7]

It is this 'responsiveness' that means that questions around when to set homework and mark work are as much about pedagogical judgement as of school policy, or at least that school policy should be more informed by pedagogical judgement than it often is.

This is not to suggest that teachers should ignore school policy, but there is a 'learned helplessness' in relying on school policy alone to determine the pedagogical choices that teachers make. Neither Ofsted, nor school leaders, want teachers to make ineffective or inefficient teaching choices because they blindly followed school policy rather than thinking for themselves about the most effective practice in their own classroom. School policy should never be a 'get out' clause for unthinking or unresponsive teaching.

As David Didau points out in *The Secret of Literacy* "no part of this sequence is really possible without any other part."[8] For example:

- Modelling of Excellence and Explaining for Understanding are intertwined and mutually reinforcing.
- Questioning as Assessment takes place across the instruction cycle.
- Testing and Retrieval as Learning occurs in episodes across the instruction cycle.
- Practice to Fluency will be interspersed with explanation, questioning and testing.

3. Reconsider the textbook

In *Why Textbooks Count*, Tim Oates advocates the use of textbooks which have the advantage of:

- Saving teachers time in producing resources.
- Reducing the "complexity" of lesson preparation.
- Allowing teachers to "focus on refining and polishing lessons."[9]

However he does decry the "narrow instrumentalism" shown by many textbooks in England, which means that these are "ranked significantly behind" those of other countries in terms of quality.[10]

And so, to the elements of instruction . . .

Ten questions for the professional practitioner to ask

Table 3.1

Question	Action
1. To what extent are my teaching judgements grounded in pedagogy?	
2. How does my planning recognise that the lesson is not the unit of learning?	
3. How do I develop medium term curriculum sequences?	
4. How does my planning take account of the 'learning' to 'learned' process?	
5. How do I ensure that my teaching is responsive?	
6. What is the relationship between my planning, instruction and assessment and is this suitably fluid and responsive?	
7. How much am I making decisions about my planning, marking, teaching and assessment (rather than over-reliance on school policy)? . . .	
8. . . . And how pedagogically grounded are these decisions?	
9. How expert am I in each of the areas of instruction?	
10. How fluidly and responsively do I use each area of instruction?	

Three ways to save time with planning

1. Save time by concentrating on the production of high quality medium term curriculum plans to map the 'learning' to 'learned' process rather than over-detailed lesson plans.
2. Save time by building more 'live' practices into instruction and assessment rather than an over-reliance on 'takeaway' assessment and feedback that is done outside the lesson.
3. Save time by reconsidering your use of high quality textbooks over teacher produced resources.

Notes

1. Allison, S. and Tharby, A. (2015) *Making Every Lesson Count*, page 9, Carmarthen, UK: Crown House
2. Husbands, C. and Pearce, J. (2012) *What Makes Great Pedagogy? Nine Claims From Research*, National College for School Leadership
3. Brown, P., Roediger III, H., and McDaniel, M. (2014) *Make it Stick: The Science of Successful Learning*, page 73, London: Harvard University Press
4. Nuthall, G. (2005) 'The Cultural Myths and Realities of Classroom Teaching and Learning: A Personal Journey' in *Teachers College Record, Volume 107*, page 928
5. Didau, D. (2015) *What if Everything You Knew About Education Was Wrong?* page 165, Carmarthen, UK: Crown House
6. Christodolou, D. (2016) *Making Good Progress? The Future of Assessment for Learning*, page 21, Oxford: Oxford University Press
7. Wiliam, D. (2016) *Leadership [for] Teaching Learning: Creating a Culture Where All Teachers Improve so That All Students Succeed*, pages 109, West Palm Beach, FL: Learning Sciences International
8. Didau, D. (2014) *The Secret of Literacy*, page 20, Carmarthen, UK: Crown House
9. Oates, T. (2014) '*Why Textbooks Count*', pages 4 and 12, Cambridge Assessment
10. Ibid. page 6

Chapter 4

Modelling of excellence

At the start of any learning process, students should 'see' what they are going to think hard about and it should be excellent.

Seeing the point

Many things in life don't benefit from being overcomplicated, and the point of the lesson is one of them.

For several years, learning objectives have been *de rigueur* in schools, in some cases reinforced with learning outcomes and success criteria. The process of 'seeing' the learning can be achieved by learning objectives, but it is important that the focus is actually on 'seeing' what the learning will look like. A lengthy list of learning objectives, learning outcomes and success criteria can lack clarity and become unwieldy and formulaic.

In *What if Everything You Knew About Education Was Wrong?* David Didau suggests that learning objectives can easily become, "a checklist of barely understood ideas that will lead only to shallow mimicry."[1]

Given that we know that learning happens when students think hard, any mindless formulae in lessons need to be considered carefully.

Classroom management formulae that allow the lesson to proceed automatically are a good idea, freeing up teacher and student working memory space to concentrate on learning; however formulaic learning strategies may not be such a good idea, as they do not promote thinking hard.

The lesson objective can also inadvertently reinforce the misconception that the lesson is the 'unit' of learning. Permanent learning occurs over sequences of lessons, and the acquisition of understanding of threshold concepts in particular may take time to acquire, as the knowledge within them may be 'troublesome' for students to reconcile with their existing schemas. This may mean a period of 'liminality' is required in which students move from one 'threshold' of understanding to another. As David Didau therefore points out, if learning objectives, "rush or limit [the liminal] ... experience then they might be doing more harm than good."[2]

It is part of the expertise of the teacher to frame difficult learning in clear language.

Five questions to ask a learning objective:

1. Is this clear?
2. Does this cause the students to think hard?
3. Does this reinforce the length of the learning process across time?
4. Does this reinforce the stage of the learning process? Are students understanding, practising, explaining, connecting, retrieving etc. in this lesson?
5. Does this capture the depth of the learning?

Why model?

We use the phrase 'I see' to indicate that we understand something.

Showing a student what learning looks like is concrete, in comparison to verbally explaining or writing down what something looks like, which is more abstract. It is this concretisation that helps students to grasp what is required more quickly and effectively; therefore saving time. As Allison and Tharby explain in *Making Every Lesson Count*, a book intended to "bridge the gap" between research and the classroom,[3] "it is hard for students to aspire to excellence if they have no inkling of what it looks like."[4]

Modelling is a step-by-step process occurring forwards, as the model is constructed, or backwards, as the model is deconstructed.

In *Principles of Instruction*, written to outline the research-based strategies that all teachers should know, Rosenshine describes modelling as a "cognitive apprenticeship" in which students learn the strategies that will develop expertise. Modelling therefore:

Provides novice learners with a way to observe 'expert thinking' that is usually hidden from the student.[5]

Ron Berger describes his expectation of students in *An Ethic of Excellence*, his argument for a paradigm shift in education to embrace excellence:

> I want my students to carry around pictures in their head of quality work. It's not enough to make a list, a rubric, of what makes a good essay or a good science experiment. This is an important step, but it doesn't leave a picture, a vision, an inspiration.[6]

Modelling also fits with the importance of 'schemas' when encoding information in the long-term memory. Didau and Rose describe a schema as "an organised framework representing some aspect of the world and a system of organising that information."[7]

Of course, some learning lends itself to the visual more than others. The expertise of the teacher is to determine how the learning can best be 'shown' to students. Rosenshine suggests models, thinking aloud and worked examples as good ways of showing outcomes to students.[8] Thinking aloud:

- Allows the student to 'see' the thinking process of the expert;
- Allows the teacher to assess the students' thought processes as they think aloud during problem-solving tasks; and[9]
- Is a quick and easy 'live' method.

In *Making Every Lesson Count*, Shaun Allison and Andy Tharby suggest the following methods in their excellent chapter on modelling:[10]

- Live writing;
- Bespoke teacher-generated models;
- Student-generated models;
- Expert models; and
- Multiple modelling of different strategies or levels of work.

The use of 'live' practices in the classroom allows the 'responsiveness' to context outlined in the last chapter as well as saving time in reducing 'takeaway' teaching practices that impinge on teachers' out-of-lesson time.

> How can I 'show' my students
> what excellence will look like?

Model everything . . .

Allison and Tharby suggest that, "we must model all parts of the learning journey, however small and seemingly insignificant, whether they are summatively assessed or not."[11] David Didau regards these 'building blocks' of learning as, "the unacknowledged repertoire of skills and knowledge an expert has available to them – the stuff we need to think with . . . if we don't tell . . . [students] what we know they'll struggle to intuit it."[12]

In *Practice Perfect* Doug Lemov *et al.* also explain the importance of modelling and describing: "If you don't tell people what to look for, they can end up observing useless things."[13]

Including mistakes . . .

And don't forget to model mistakes. In *Principles of Instruction*, Rosenshine points out that effective teachers are able to anticipate students' errors.[14] By 'modelling' likely errors in advance, teachers can save both themselves and their students' time and help students to form correct schemas from the start, rather than needing to spend extra time in re-teaching to correct errors.

Thinking not learning?

We use the word 'learning' a lot in teaching: Learning objectives, learning outcomes, We Are Learning To, What I Have Learned Today?

Is it worth considering more use of the word 'thinking?'

Learning is an invisible and long-term process. We cannot easily tell whether we are learning, and the moment that knowledge transfers from 'learning' to 'learned' is also invisible to us. In contrast, we can tell more easily when we are thinking hard about something.

This is not mere pedantry. Cognitive science indicates that we can mistake what effective learning looks like. This brings us back to the point made by Brown *et al.* that "we are poor judges of when we are learning well."[15]

'Thinking hard' about the point of the lesson is easier to explain, model and evaluate than 'learning,' as well as being a better predictor of effective learning. An OECD report, published in 2011, *Against the Odds: Disadvantaged Students Who Succeed in School*[16] found that resilient learners are 'mentally present' in class. Similarly, in the Model of School Learning developed by Caroll,[17] he links learning explicitly to time spent actively on task – in other words 'thinking hard.'

Fluency not learning?

Chapter 2 described the learning process as:

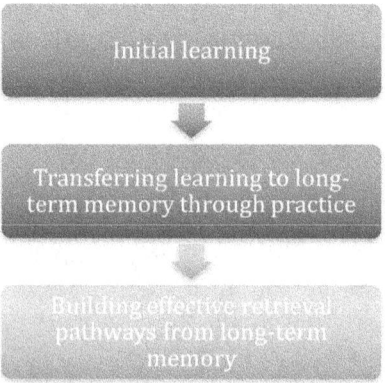

Fluency fits within this:

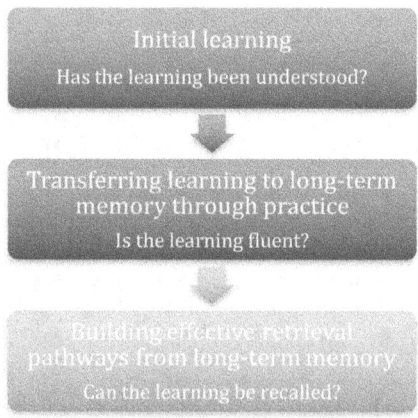

'Fluency' is one of those words that, 'does what it says on the tin.' I cannot tell whether I have learned something immediately because whether it is 'learned' relies on my ability to recall it at a later date. I cannot necessarily tell whether I have understood something until I have been able to practise it correctly; however I can tell whether I am fluent in learning if I am able to do something correctly, repeatedly and automatically.

Even more than the word 'mastery,' the word 'fluency' has a benchmark built in.

In order to have fully 'mastered' propositional or procedural knowledge, we need to be 'fluent' in it. Fluency implies understanding, expertise, speed, and automaticity. As one student commented in my school – it's not when you get it right, but when you can't get it wrong.

Therefore lesson objectives focused on the acquisition of 'fluency' will lead logically to thought by the teacher and student about what the journey to 'fluency' looks like.

It is important that students understand the three-part process of the journey from 'learning' to 'learned,' otherwise they may assume that initial understanding is the full learning process.

The answer to "what have I learned today" is actually often – if again somewhat earnestly: "Nothing; however you have begun the learning process by gaining initial understanding." This is because the lesson is not the unit of total learning, which goes through a process of:

1. Understanding;
2. Practising to fluency; and
3. Effective recalling and retrieval to embed permanency.

This process will take place over a series of lessons and we should be careful not to lull students, or ourselves, into a false sense of security that learning has occurred at stage 1 or even stage 2 when, without stage 3, in a few weeks 'learning' will have melted away.

How much do students get wrong because they don't know, and how much do they get wrong because they once knew but don't any more?

It is for the teacher to decide what students need to understand and practise to fluency:

- Are students gaining fluency in a body of knowledge?
- Are students gaining fluency in understanding of a concept?
- Are students gaining technical proficiency?

Of course the word 'skills' can be substituted for 'proficiency' but 'skills' has become a loaded word in teaching, bound up in the knowledge versus skills debate. There is also a 'fluidity' in our use of the word 'skills,' which is often used in education as a noun (we are improving our source work skills today,) rather than a verb (I am skilled in the technique of source work.) 'Proficiency' is another 'Ronseal' word: It 'does what it says on the tin.' If I am not 'proficient' in something, by definition, I am not fluent in it. The benchmark is built into the word. Once again, focus on 'proficiency' leads logically to thought about what 'proficiency' looks like.

Using what we know about effective learning, a suitable objective might therefore be:

> Thinking hard about X to become fluent at Y

Or:

> Thinking hard about X to become proficient in Y

Or the learning objective might reflect the stage of the learning journey:

> Ultimate aim: To be fluent in X
> Stage in the learning journey: Y

Why excellence?

- **Because education should be about excellence:** No school aspires to 'Education for Mediocrity.' It is worth quoting from Ron Berger's book *An Ethic of Excellence* on the subject of excellence, although this is a poor substitute for the inspiration

to be gained from reading the book itself. Berger writes: "I want a classroom full of craftsmen. I want students whose work is strong and accurate and beautiful."[18]
- **Because work of excellence is transformational:** Berger believes that, "once a student sees that he or she is capable of excellence, that student is never quite the same."[19]
- **Because excellence denotes value:** Berger reminds us that, "it's easy to see what is valued in a culture by looking at which structures are built with expense and care."[20] If our students are to grasp that education is valuable, this must be reinforced by the emphasis that we place as teachers on 'care-full' work.
- Because ambition for excellence drives improvement: Berger argues that:

> The most important assessment that goes on in a school ... goes on *inside* students. Every student walks around the school with a picture of what is acceptable, what is good enough ... How do we get inside students' heads and turn up the knob that regulates quality and effort?[21]

- **Because excellence should be inherent:** One of the pressures on teachers has been the effect of trying to juggle a number of balls and squeeze these into their teaching, including 'Stretch and Challenge.' By setting excellence as a benchmark, high expectation is incorporated into teachers' thinking about the learning process rather than being an extra add-on that might be forgotten, or just applied for 'more able' students.

What is excellence?

Be ambitious

In *An Ethic of Excellence*, Ron Berger argues that "the key to excellence is this: It is born from a culture."[22]

We do need to think instrumentally as teachers. Excellence may well be visualised as a particular grade or level of work, or work that would mean that students were making excellent progress; however there are other types of excellence to consider:

- The best that has been thought or said;
- The nub of the subject; and
- Threshold concepts or proficiencies.

In *The Secret of Literacy*, David Didau writes about teaching English:

> How much more effort would it have taken to provide examples from Dickens or Hardy? How much more benefit might have been accrued if I'd used an article from *The Times* or *The Guardian* instead of the *Daily Mail*? The reason for not doing this, in the past, was that I believed it was sufficient to focus on the skills of writing and neglected many opportunities for enriching my pupils with some of the more challenging texts out there.[23]

Quality over quantity

Ron Berger criticises "school treadmills that focus on quantity of work rather than quality of work ... a piece of work that is not ready in one draft carries the stigma of weakness or failure [yet] what could you possibly achieve of quality in a single draft?"[24]

Learning, and therefore excellence, is content-dependent. We cannot learn something without learning something!

In subjects, our learning will probably take one of two forms:

1. Learning of propositional knowledge and concepts: Knowledge that; and
2. Learning of procedural knowledge: Knowledge of how to.

In *Knowledge and the Future School*, Young and Lambert argue against the "evacuation of content"[25] in education, especially for those not already succeeding in school. As outlined in Chapter 1, they see 'powerful' knowledge as a framework for constructing curricula, but it may also be a useful definition when considering excellence.

Excellence is inclusive

In *Becoming a High Expectation Teacher*, Rubie-Davies finds evidence over several years of research into teacher expectation effect that teacher expectations, "influence student performance and achievement ... Teacher expectations become closely aligned with both the instructional and psychosocial environment of the classroom, and this intensifies the likelihood that the students' behaviour will become more aligned with the expectation."[26]

Rubie-Davies suggests that teachers' expectations of their students have an influence on their pedagogical choices:

> As a result of what teachers have planned for student learning, they will implement learning experiences for students based on their expectations and their pedagogical beliefs about what is appropriate for students of perceived variable ability ... Students then participate in the learning experiences provided by the teacher and learn as a result of what is offered. An important point, therefore, is that students learn what they have been given the opportunity to learn.[27]

It is for this reason that Rubie-Davies finds that, "low differentiation is a practice that is common among high expectation teachers."[28]

High expectation teachers give all their students more opportunities to learn rather than creating 'differentiated' learning opportunities that have the unintended impact of restricting the learning opportunities of some groups of students. The accumulation of these high or low expectation pedagogical choices can have a significant impact over time.

Rubie-Davies also suggests that where teachers have high expectations of students they are more likely to persevere with teaching strategies when they are not initially successful, but where they believe lack of success to be caused due to lack of ability by students they are more likely to give up: "This is because teachers are not always confident about how they should respond when students do not learn new concepts quickly and are likely to look for different pedagogical approaches when students fail to learn."[29]

Similarly in *Learning Without Limits*, Susan Hart et al. argue for 'transformability': "The belief that, "all children's capacity to learn can change and be changed for the better as a result of what happens and what people do in the present."[30]

In a piece on 'myth busting' posted on *Class Teaching*, the Durrington High School blog, in 2014, Shaun Allison suggests that learning objectives that start with 'all, most, some' are unhelpful:

> I think they stifle aspirations of what students can achieve and give them an easy way out – 'I'll just focus on the All objective and not bother about the rest.' Much better to have a single, challenging objective for all and support all students to aspire to get there.[31]

David Didau agrees that differentiated learning intentions and success criteria based on grades can lead to students and teachers "anchoring themselves on data never intended for this purpose and which gives tacit permission for low expectations."[32]

Every child deserves to be taught to fluency in what they are learning; otherwise we condemn some of our students to the perpetual twilight of being 'partial' or 'emerging', like early amphibians.

Ron Berger writes movingly about the production of excellence by a student with learning difficulties:

> Five minutes ago . . . [the audience] saw just another project by an anonymous, talented kid. Now the struggle, work, and growth that this project represented was evident.[33]

Tim Oates also joins the 'excellence for all' bandwagon, pointing out in '*Why Textbooks Count*' that in Shanghai, Singapore, Japan and Finland, understanding of ability, and therefore differentiation, is very different to England:

> All children are assumed to be capable of understanding, and ideas are elaborated in different ways in order to encourage individual understanding.[34]

We need to ask ourselves the question, do we think that our students cannot achieve excellence, or do we think that they are not prepared to put in the hard work to achieve excellence?

De-construct excellence

If achieving excellence was simply a case of showing students 'excellence' for them to reproduce, teaching would be much quicker and easier (although also less interesting and challenging.) By its very nature, excellence can appear 'finished' and inaccessible. The definition of fluency is synonymous with words that run counter to the actual learning experience: Smooth, effortless, easy, natural.

For those of a certain generation, *Blue Peter* provides a practical answer: De-construction. Its presenters would take us through a learning process by producing a series of deconstructed 'here's one I made earlier' models that gradually constructed an outcome.

Deconstruct through worked examples . . .

The skill of the teacher is to deconstruct excellence into its component parts. Researchers refer to 'worked examples,' which provide step-by-step demonstrations of how to perform a task or solve a problem and the underlying principles beneath these steps.

A note of caution

Allison and Tharby rightly warn that

> bad modelling can be akin to spoon-feeding; if it over-dominates it can lead to the teacher doing the cognitive work that the student should be doing themselves. This is why it is so important to regularly put models to one side and allow students to struggle for themselves.[35]

Similarly, in *The Secret of Literacy*, David Didau argues that overuse of scaffolds and writing frames "often result in formulaic writing which slavishly follows a structure with little understanding of the processes and thinking involved . . . We must always keep in mind the consideration of when to withdraw support."[36]

In *Principles of Instruction*, Rosenshine avoids this by proposing a three-step model:[37]

> Provide a prompt, model or worked example

> Model the use of the prompt, model or worked example

> Guide students to independence from this

Ten questions for the professional practitioner to ask

Table 4.1

Question	Action
1. How am I using my learning objectives to enhance students' thinking hard and understanding the learning process?	
2. How am I using modelling in my teaching?	
3. How am I getting students to focus on thinking hard in my lessons?	
4. How am I ensuring that students understand the process from 'learning' to 'learned'?	
5. Is my teaching building fluency? For all learners?	
6. How do my classroom climate and lesson planning promote excellence? For all learners?	
7. Am I being sufficiently ambitious for my learners? All of them?	
8. Are my curricular choices sufficiently 'powerful' and ambitious?	
9. How am I using deconstruction in my teaching?	
10. How am I ensuring that students are able to work successfully without models?	

Twelve ways to save time with modelling of excellence

Save time spent thinking up and writing learning objectives

1. Use more simple learning objectives focused on all students acquiring fluency.
2. Use models rather than learning objectives so that students can 'see' the learning outcome.

In *Teaching: Notes From the Front Line*, published in 2014, Debra Kidd calculated that students could be spending 32.5 hours a year writing down learning objectives.[38]

Save lesson time

3. Use models to save time in the lesson and ensure that students comprehend more quickly, and use less of their working memory space.

In *Principles of Instruction* Rosenshine points out that worked examples and models can save time in the learning process by reducing the cognitive load on students' working memories.[39] In comparison, Daniel Willingham points out that the following techniques overload working memory:

- Multi-step instructions (remember that working memory can process, on average, four chunks of information at a time);
- Lists of unconnected information; and
- Chains of logic that are more than one or two steps long.[40]

Save time spent creating new resources

4. Build up banks of models.
5. Use past and present students' work to model both excellence and misconceptions.
6. Don't be afraid to use models from the textbook.

Save time spent giving written feedback

7. Use models as feedback.

Shaun Allison and Andy Tharby point out that using models as exemplars for students to compare their work against gives "a potentially richer, quicker and more detailed form of feedback than a written comment."[41]

8. Model errors before setting work so that you eliminate these from the start and therefore reduce feedback time.
9. Assess students' learning using 'live' thinking aloud techniques that save time and allow you to give powerful 'on the spot' verbal feedback.

Save time spent planning 'add ons' into your lessons

10. Stop thinking of stretch and challenge as an, 'add on' or extension task and integrate it into your lessons. To 'add in' stretch

challenge as an extension tasks implies that the previous tasks were not stretching and challenging.

Save time spent on differentiation

11. Don't use differentiation that condemns some students to partial knowledge, restricted learning opportunities or permanent mediocrity.

Save time in the long term

12. By investing the time in high expectations of students; save time and effort as your students 'raise their game.'

Where does modelling fit in the instruction sequence?

Obviously modelling plays a crucial role in giving students initial understanding, but it can also be used across the instruction sequence:

- Models can be used to elucidate explanation;
- Models can be used to guide practice;
- Models can be used as assessment benchmarks of excellence; and
- Models can be used as exemplars that close the feedback loop.

Notes

1. Didau, D. (2015) *What if Everything You Knew About Education Was Wrong?* pages 278–279, Carmarthen, UK: Crown House
2. Ibid. page 279
3. Allison, S. and Tharby, A. (2015) *Making Every Lesson Count*, front cover sleeve, Carmarthen, UK: Crown House
4. Ibid. page 25
5. Rosenshine, B. (2012) 'Principles of Instruction: Research-Based Strategies That All Teachers Should Know' in *American Education, spring 2012*, page 18
6. Berger, R. (2003) *An Ethic of Excellence*, page 83, Portsmouth, NH: Heinemann
7. Didau, D. and Rose, N. (2016) *What Every Teacher Needs to Know About . . . Psychology*, page 19, Woodbridge, UK: John Catt
8. Rosenshine, B. (2012) 'Principles of Instruction: Research-Based Strategies That All Teachers Should Know' in *American Education, spring 2012*, page 15

9. Ibid. page 16
10. Allison, S. and Tharby, A. (2015) *Making Every Lesson Count*, pages 89–122, Carmarthen, UK: Crown House
11. Ibid. page 115
12. Didau, D. (2015) *What if Everything You Knew About Education Was Wrong?* page 164, Carmarthen, UK: Crown House
13. Lemov, D., Woolway, E. and Yezzi, K. (2012) *Practice Perfect: 42 Rules for Getting Better and Better*, page 88, San Francisco, CA: Jossey Bass
14. Rosenshine, B. (2012) 'Principles of Instruction: Research-Based Strategies That All Teachers Should Know' in *American Education, spring 2012*, page 18
15. Brown, P., Roediger III, H., and McDaniel, M. (2014) *Make it Stick: The Science of Successful Learning*, page 3, London: Harvard University Press
16. www.oecd.org/edu/school/programmeforinternationalstudentassessment pisa/pisaagainsttheoddsdisadvantagedstudentswhosucceedinschool.htm
17. http://edutechwiki.unige.ch/en/Carroll_model_of_school_learning
18. Berger, R. (2003) *An Ethic of Excellence*, page 1, Portsmouth, NH: Heinemann
19. Ibid. page 8
20. Ibid. page 46
21. Ibid. page 103
22. Ibid. page 6
23. Didau, D. (2014) *The Secret of Literacy*, page 36, Carmarthen, UK: Crown House
24. Berger, R. (2003) *An Ethic of Excellence*, pages 9 and 89–90, Portsmouth, NH: Heinemann
25. Young, M. and Lambert, D. with Roberts, C. and Roberts, M. (2015) *Knowledge and the Future School*, page 90, London: Bloomsbury
26. Rubie-Davies, R. (2015) *Becoming a High Expectation Teacher: Raising the Bar,* pages xiv and xv, Abingdon, UK: Routledge
27. Ibid. page 15
28. Ibid. page xvi
29. Ibid. pages 35–36
30. Hart, S., Dixon, A., Drummond, M., and McIntyre, D. (2004) Learning Without Limits, page 166, Maidenhead, UK: Open University Press
31. https://classteaching.wordpress.com/2014/09/13/mythbusting/
32. Didau, D. (2015) *What if Everything You Knew About Education Was Wrong?* pages 280, Carmarthen, UK: Crown House
33. Berger, R. (2003) *An Ethic of Excellence*, page 23, Portsmouth, NH: Heinemann
34. Oates, T. (2014) '*Why Textbooks Count*', page 12, Cambridge Assessment
35. Allison, S. and Tharby, A. (2015) *Making Every Lesson Count*, pages 119, Carmarthen, UK: Crown House
36. Didau, D. (2014) *The Secret of Literacy*, page 39 and 46, Carmarthen, UK: Crown House

37. Rosenshine, B. (2012) 'Principles of Instruction: Research-Based Strategies That All Teachers Should Know' in *American Education, spring 2012*, page 14
38. Kidd, D. (2014) *Teaching: Notes from the Front Line*, Carmarthen, UK: Crown House
39. Rosenshine, B. (2012) 'Principles of Instruction: Research-Based Strategies That All Teachers Should Know' in *American Education, spring 2012*, page 14
40. Willingham, D. (2009) *Why Don't Students Like School?*, page 20, San Francisco, CA: Jossey-Bass
41. Allison, S. and Tharby, A. (2015) *Making Every Lesson Count*, page 114, Carmarthen, UK: Crown House

Chapter 5

Explaining for understanding

Even if learners are clear about what they need to think about, their learning will not progress if they do not understand it or cannot process it.

Explanation therefore plays a vital, and arguably underestimated, role both in elucidating learning, and connecting it, and thereby facilitating the transfer of learning to long-term memory.

The role of explanation in the process of 'learning' to 'learned':

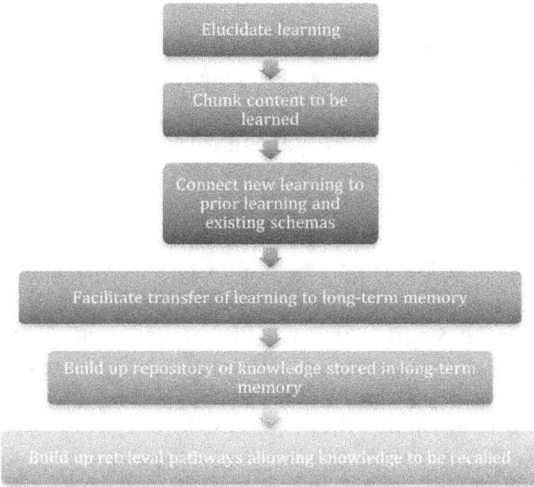

Lee Shulman suggests in *Knowledge and Teaching* that the teacher explains by:

- Talking;
- Showing;

- Enacting; and
- Representing ideas.[1]

He argues that for teaching to occur, the knowledge to be understood must be "transformed" in some way, rather than merely transmitted. This theory explains why students cannot simply autodidact from the internet. This 'transformation' requires a number of pedagogical choices to be made by the teacher including:

- How to adapt materials;
- How to construct multiple representations to explain the knowledge (for example, analogies metaphors, examples, demonstrations and simulations); and
- What instructional selections to make from a range of teaching methods.

All of the above should be adapted to the general and specific characteristics of the group of students to be taught.[2]

By this definition, explanation is a profoundly responsive process in which teacher judgement of the specific classroom context and the range of explanatory tools available is crucial to high quality teacher performance.

Despite this, the importance of explanation has been underplayed in professional learning in recent years.

Ofsted's dislike for 'teacher talk' has meant that the objective of explanation has been brevity over clarity, with teachers engaging in surreptitious 'chalk and talk' lessons when lengthy explanation is needed, and students begging for 'off the record' explanation. In *The Secret of Literacy*, David Didau points out that, "this insanity has led to teachers showcasing lessons that don't require pupils to know anything beyond their own life experiences. And this leads, inexorably, to setting tasks with very low expectations."[3]

Picking up on this theme in *What if Everything You Knew About Education Was Wrong?* Didau decries the "toxic effect" that the restriction on teacher talk has had, in particular on the ability of teachers to model academic language in the classroom. As he says, "if students are actually going to learn anything worthwhile, teachers absolutely must talk." [4]

Far from teacher talk being an unnecessary and distracting adjunct to student learning, Kirschner *et al.* explain in *Why Minimal Guidance in Instruction Does Not Work*, that actually unguided instruction is less effective and can result in students acquiring misconceptions.⁵

The importance of effective explanation is reinforced when we consider that students learn information by creating schemas. Teacher explanation obviously plays a crucial part in the development of correct schemas.

Sticky explanation

For explanation to be effective, it needs to be memorable. In *Teaching that Sticks*, an article to support their longer book on the subject, Chip and Dan Heath point out that 'sticky' explanations "share common traits."⁶ The effectiveness of 'sticky' explanation explains the success of some 'chalk and talk' teachers, which has long posed a perplexing and irritating mystery to proponents of 'activity learning.'

The traits of 'sticky explanations':

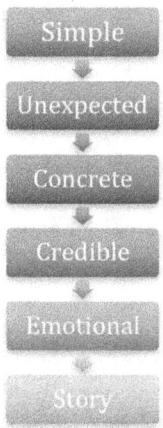

Sticky explanation is simple

Keep explanation focused. Chip and Dan Heath suggest that, "some concepts are more critical than others."⁷ Of obvious importance is the explanation of any threshold concepts that provide a gateway to deeper understanding.

Simplicity can also be provided by a clear learning objective focused on students thinking hard about meaning and expressed in academically rigorous but crystal clear, concise and repetitious language that hammers home the points to be understood – ideally reinforced by appropriate non-verbal language. Daniel Willingham points out that as "ninety five per cent of what students learn in school concerns meaning . . . a teacher's goal should almost always be to get students to think about meaning."[8] He asks: "Instead of making the work easier, is it possible to make the thinking easier?"[9]

Simplicity can also be provided through effective chunking of information. Chunking both connects information within students' schemas and ensures effective use of the limited space in working memory. A good example is our use of words. As one word, 'memory' is easier to remember than the six separate letters m-e-m-o-r-y. Words 'chunk' and create meaning out of what would otherwise be random letters; which is why mnemonics can be an effective learning tool.

Sticky explanation is unexpected

Chip and Dan Heath suggest that, "piquing curiosity is the holy grail of teaching."[10] This can be done in the following ways:

- Creating knowledge gaps: Curiosity arises when we feel a gap in our knowledge;
- Making predictions which engage students and induce curiosity; and
- Picking unusual or unexpected analogies that cause students to think hard.

Sticky explanation is concrete

As mentioned in the previous chapter, we use the phrase 'I see' to indicate that we understand something. Effective explanation allows the learner to 'see' what they are learning – it 'paints the picture'. For this reason, good explanation is able to elucidate and 'familiarise' new learning.

Young and Lambert argue that 'powerful knowledge' should take students beyond their experience, introducing them to, "concepts, which have meanings that do not derive from or relate directly to their experience."[11] In the acquisition of 'powerful knowledge' therefore, being able to link this 'un-experienced' learning to the familiar is all the more important.

Daniel Willingham points out that, "it's not the concreteness; it's the familiarity that's important."[12]

This familiarity can be created using the following methods:

- Concretise;
- Analogise to the familiar;
- Model; and
- Exemplify by:
  i. Giving a range of positive examples of a concept;
  ii. Giving the limits of the concept by negative examples; and
  iii. Giving minimally different examples.

Didau and Rose explain that explanations such as analogies can be used as part of the process of "anchoring new, abstract ideas to . . . [the] concrete and familiar ideas students already possess."[13] They argue that because the culturally constructed 'secondary' knowledge that students need to learn in schools is so abstract, the ability of teachers to create connections for students between concrete and abstract representations of the same concept is important: "Developing good explanations and accurate analogies is probably the key area of subject specialist knowledge teachers most need to develop."[14]

It is important that, once grasped, explanations are 'transposed' into the necessary specialist academic register. David Didau warns against allowing students to use, "sloppy, imprecise language."[15] Similarly, Shaun Allison and Andy Tharby emphasise the need to "model and promote more complex academic language as you move from surface to deep learning."[16]

Sticky explanation is credible

Chip and Dan Heath point out that, "For an idea to stick, it needs to be credible."[17]

Developing the habit of using knowledge to make explanation credible is important, as knowledge plays a vital role in expert learning.

In *Domain-Specific Knowledge*, Tricot and Sweller argue that where cognitive activities require domain-specific knowledge, "the presence or absence of this knowledge is the best predictor of performance."[18] This explains their findings that low-aptitude experts can outperform high-aptitude novices.[19]

As we know from Chapter 2, the limited capacity of working memory only applies to new and unfamiliar information; therefore when students have prior domain-specific knowledge it improves the capacity of their working memory. In an article on cognitive load, Renkl and Atkinson explain that the *intrinsic* cognitive load of any learning material is actually dependent on prior domain-specific knowledge: "High-prior knowledge allows for constructing larger meaningful information chunks so that cognitive load is reduced."[20]

Therefore the complexity of any content is relative to the student's level of prior knowledge of that content.

Daniel Willingham points out that background knowledge also speeds up learning because it facilitates the 'chunking' process: For chunking to occur we must have sufficient understanding to see how information can be meaningfully chunked, i.e. to convert m-e-m-o-r-y into 'memory,' this word must have some meaning. This 'chunking' in turn creates space in the working memory for new learning.[21] Background knowledge also improves understanding of new domain knowledge, and therefore speeds up the acquisition of new learning, which can be more easily assimilated into 'stronger' existing schemas.

Sticky explanation provokes emotion

Chip and Dan Heath point out that ideas that "make people feel something" are more easily retained.[22] The emotion might be inherent in the idea, or connected to the explanation of the idea.

Sticky explanation tells a story

Daniel Willingham explains that stories are powerful because they are "psychologically privileged."[23] This is because they contain the key features of good explanation:

- They are easy to understand;
- They contain a recognised structure;
- They are interesting;
- They are easy to remember; and
- They focus thinking on meaning.

Didau and Rose wonder whether this is because they "tap into the episodic processes which underpin the beginnings of semantic memory."[24]

It is therefore worth considering how we build these six key features of 'sticky' explanation into our explanations.

Four elements of explanation in the instruction sequence:

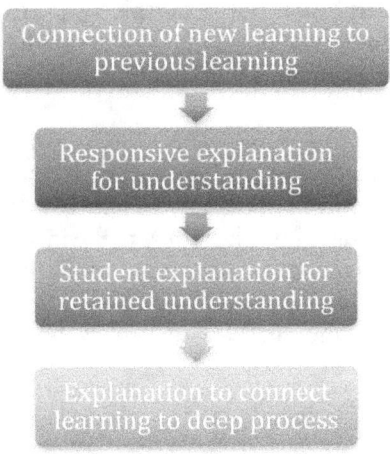

Element 1: Connection of new learning to previous learning

We understand new information most quickly in the context of information that we already know. The more effectively it can be explained to fit with our existing schemas of understanding, the more quickly it will be assimilated.

In *Make it Stick*, Brown *et al.* explain that, "all new learning requires a foundation of prior knowledge ... [and] there's virtually no limit to how much learning we can remember as long as we relate it to what we already know."[25]

This is why familiar analogies are such a powerful explanation tool and, therefore, an important part of the teacher's repertoire.

Daniel Willingham points out that they help us to understand something new by relating it to something we already know about: "Understanding new ideas is mostly a matter of getting the right old ideas into working memory."[26]

Elimination of misconceptions

An important element of initial explanation is teacher pedagogical content knowledge of the common misconceptions that students acquire in a subject so that the schemas that they build are correct from the start. This will save time in unpicking acquired misconceptions.

Didau and Rose point out that this is particularly necessary when culturally constructed secondary knowledge appears to contradict biological primary knowledge, i.e. it involves 'threshold concepts.'[27]

Rosenshine explains in *Principles of Instruction* that often students can acquire misconceptions as they connect new knowledge to their existing schemas; this can occur particularly when students' background knowledge is weak so they make incorrect assumptions. Rosenshine believes that these errors are more likely to occur if the teacher presents too much new information at once with insufficient checking for understanding.[28]

Explanation as transposition

To 'transpose' is to transfer to a different place or context; in music this refers to the process of moving a collection of notes up or down in pitch. In explanation the teacher undertakes a process of transposition (the analogy of limbo dancing often comes to my mind as I sometimes wonder how low I need to go!) In the process of explanation, the teacher transposes down to 'hook' students' comprehension and then transposes back up the scale again in terms of both conceptual understanding and academic register of language.

Element 2: Responsive explanation for understanding

One of the reasons that explanation went out of fashion was that, in an era of 'visible progress,' it was harder for observers to 'see' learning than when students were engaged in independent practice. That parts of the learning process are invisible does not invalidate them, however the problem of evaluating the impact of explanation can be overcome, to some extent, by responsive explanation, which allows the teacher to track the learning occurring during explanation more accurately.

In *Principles of Instruction*, Rosenshine advocates teachers presenting new material in small steps including many concrete examples, and use of elaboration with student practice after each step.[29] This both:

- Acknowledges the limits of students' working memories; and
- Allows the teacher to monitor the impact of explanation and respond accordingly.

Rosenshine's findings are worth examining because they contradict the prohibition on teacher talk that became common in many English schools during the era of 'activity' learning.

He found that, "the more effective teachers spent more time presenting new material and guiding student practice than did the less effective teachers" – in the cases that he observed, effective teachers spent over half the lesson in forms of 'teacher talk.' In one effective lesson seen, this amounted to 58 per cent of the lesson time spent on lecture, demonstration, questioning and worked examples, compared to 28 per cent of the lesson time in a less effective lesson seen. This additional 'teacher talk' time was spent on providing sufficient explanation and checking of student understanding of explanation. This then allowed students to work independently more successfully, therefore reducing the amount of teacher support needed compared to the less effective lessons in which explanations were shorter.[30]

Rosenshine therefore suggests a responsive model of:

- Explanation;
- Demonstration;
- Checking for understanding; and
- Guided instruction through worked examples.

In *Making Every Lesson Count*, Shaun Allison and Andy Tharby provide another of their useful lists of ideas and strategies for encouraging responsive explanation, including to:

- Communicate with your body language;
- Feel your words;
- Ask students to repeat your words; and
- Use "razor-sharp" instructions.[31]

Element 3: Student explanation for retained understanding

It is important that teacher explanation, however responsive, is followed by student self-explanation, otherwise students can mistake the fluency of the teacher's explanation with their own fluency of understanding.

It is also important to stress that self-explanation is not the same as student explanation.

This chapter has not achieved its purpose if it has not demonstrated the knowledge and expertise involved in effective explanation. It is also worth noting Graham Nuthall's findings that 80 per cent of the feedback students get on their work from each other is wrong.[32]

There are two types of student explanation:

- Elaborative interrogation; and
- Self-explanation.

Elaborative explanation is the process of giving new material meaning by expressing it in your own words and connecting it with what you already know.

> Why would this fact be true of X but not of Y

Dunlosky *et al.* found that elaborative interrogation activities helped students to connect new learning to existing prior knowledge. These 'explanatory' activities were more effective:

- The more precise the elaborations were;
- The greater the students' prior knowledge; and
- The more self-generated the elaborations were.[33]

Self-explanation involves students explaining their processing during problem-solving or procedural tasks (this could be written down or done 'live' aloud.) In *Improving Students' Learning With Effective Learning Techniques*, Dunlosky *et al.* suggest that self-explanation may help learning as (like elaborate interrogation) a means by which new information can be integrated with students' existing prior knowledge.[34]

In *Make it Stick*, Brown *et al.* explain that self-explanation connecting new learning to prior knowledge both increases understanding of the new learning and creates connections that help this to be remembered. For teachers, listening to self-explanation also provides a strategy for assessing students' understanding.[35]

Element 4: Explanation to connect learning to deep process

New knowledge that students learn exists in connection to both their prior knowledge, and the deep principles that underlie this knowledge. Once information has been explained for understanding, it is therefore important that this new knowledge is 'connected up' to students' larger frameworks of knowledge.

Explanation for retrieval: Encoding and creating cues

We should be mindful that for information to become 'learned' rather than 'learning' it will need to be both storable and retrievable. **In order to store information effectively we need to encode it.**

Brown *et al.* explain that, "people who learn to extract the key ideas from new material and organise them into a mental model and connect that model to prior knowledge show an advantage in learning complex mastery."[36]

Similarly, the report *Teaching Adolescents To Become Learners* found that the most effective learning strategies involved manipulating and organising material, for example:

- Connecting new information and prior knowledge;
- Creating elaborative structures; and
- Transforming information into meaningful schemata.[37]

In his *Evidence Into Practice* blog, Nick Rose cites research by Bower *et al.* that, "semantic, hierarchical organisation of material greatly aided recall."[38]

However, he also warns against the danger of inaccurate encoding which can *reduce* recall when students assign key concepts into inappropriate semantic groups. Nick Rose warns that, "mind mapping without a secure understanding of a topic might simply consolidate any misconceptions that exist or lead to the material being 'organised' in a fairly arbitrary way."[39]

In *What if Everything You Knew About Education Was Wrong?* David Didau suggests that, to avoid this, the "tediously familiar" common encoding errors need to be addressed in teaching.[40]

We then need to be able to retrieve it.

Daniel Willingham points out that, "remembering things is all about cues to memory."[41] Brown *et al.* explain that, "we must associate the material [to be learned] with a diverse set of cues that will make us adept at recalling the knowledge later. Having effective retrieval cues is an aspect of learning that often goes overlooked."[42]

Time saving explanation

In *What Every Teacher Needs to Know About ... Psychology*, Didau and Rose suggest that we can expand the capacity of working memory by explaining visual and auditory information simultaneously without adding to cognitive load.[43] They advise that explanation through a joint visual and verbal presentation, rather than a verbal and written presentation that places more strain on working memory, is a technique that teachers should "regularly exploit."[44]

Didau and Rose suggest reducing extraneous cognitive load by using the following techniques:

- Removing unnecessary information: Written and visual;
- Highlighting important information;
- Combining written and visual information;
- Ensuring that oral explanation matches visual information;
- Reducing the amount of attention switching that students need to do in looking at different sources of information; and
- Using visual images that 'show' the organisation, relationships, processes or connections that students need to understand.

Their chapter on how to design effective instructional materials is definitely worth reading.[45]

Explaining for understanding 89

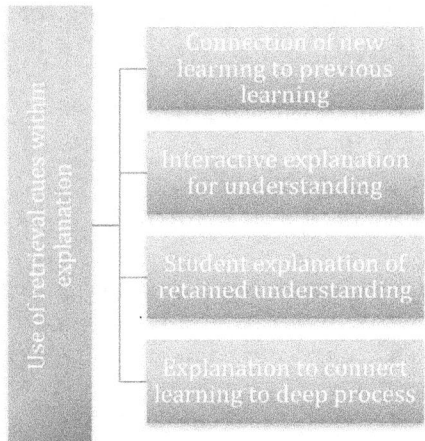

Ten questions for the professional practitioner to ask

Table 5.1

Question	Action
1. What explanation techniques am I using?	
2. How am I chunking explanation to ensure that students' working memories are not overloaded?	
3. How do I insist on a high level of academic oracy?	
4. How do I build students' domain knowledge?	
5. How do I connect student learning to both prior knowledge and 'deep structure' knowledge?	
6. What are the common misconceptions in my subject and how do I identify and address these?	
7. How do I get students to use self-explanation and elaborative explanation?	
8. How do I ensure that students are correctly encoding knowledge?	
9. How do I build students' retrieval pathways through my explanations?	
10. How do I reduce extraneous cognitive load in my presentations?	

Fifteen ways to save time with explaining for understanding

Save learning time in present and future lessons by creating 'cognitive short cuts'

1. Chunk your explanation so that you create more room in students' working memories to process the learning more quickly.
2. Encode your explanation as you go so that students are encoding information correctly to reduce time spent on correcting misconceptions later, and to facilitate the transfer of learning to long-term memory.
3. Develop 'visible' schemas to help students to 'see' how the learning connects.
4. Build in retrieval cues to explanation as you go so that students are building up their retrieval pathways to save 'revision' time later on.
5. Consider the timing of initial explanations. For example, initial explanation towards the end of a lesson allows the learning to be introduced by you the expert, and allows the correcting of key misconceptions, but can then be supplemented with further investigation through flipped learning by students; thereby reducing the amount of time spent in lesson on initial explanation.
6. Consider how your medium term curriculum sequences build up student domain knowledge over time. The more knowledge that students have, the quicker and more effectively they will learn.

Save time by using high quality explanation and 'teacher talk'

7. Instead of sourcing and producing resources, use high quality 'live' explanations, bespoke for the group in front of you.
8. Use Rosenshine's strategy of intertwined explanation and practice to:
    i. Prevent overloading students' working memory;
    ii. Assess the impact of initial explanation so that you can respond accordingly; and
    iii. Reduce time spent on supporting student practice because the initial explanation was not thorough enough.

9. Instead of written feedback, deliver 'live' feedback and explanation.
10. Instead of producing differentiated resources, differentiate 'live' through on-the-spot explanations.
11. Instead of wasting lesson time on student 'discovery' and explanation tasks, 'cut to the chase.' Start with clear and concise teacher explanation and then spend more time on student self-explanations. Both will save you time because they do not need to be supported by extensive resources.

Save time by building up resources

12. Build up shared banks of misconceptions, positive and negative examples, stories and analogies.
13. Make presentations more effective and efficient by using the strategies for preparing instruction materials outlined by David Didau and Nick Rose.

Save learning time by insisting on high quality student oracy

14. Use your oracy and your students' oracy in lessons to develop academic vocabulary.
15. Use 'live' student self-explanations to assess students' understanding. The oral feedback that you can give on these is quicker, more immediate and more impactful than written feedback.

Where does explanation fit in the instruction sequence?

Explanation plays an obvious role in the acquisition of initial understanding, but it should also be used across the instruction sequence in order to explain:

- Models;
- Practice;
- Assessment;
- Tests; and
- Feedback.

The beauty of explanation from a time saving point of view is that powerfully articulated 'live' explanation is more effective than written explanation. Explanation should also be part of a cycle of 'responsive' teaching, for example, explain model, practice, assess, explain feedback.

Notes

1. Shulman, L. (1987) 'Knowledge and Teaching: Foundations of the New Reform' in *Harvard Educational Review, Volume 57*, page 7, Harvard College
2. Ibid. pages 16–17
3. Didau, D. (2014) *The Secret of Literacy*, pages 57–58, Carmarthen, UK: Crown House
4. Didau, D. (2015) *What if Everything You Knew About Education Was Wrong?* page 79, Carmarthen, UK: Crown House
5. Kirschner, P., Sweller, J. and Clark, R. (2006) 'Why Minimal Guidance During Instruction Does Not Work: An Analysis of the Failure of Constructivist, Discovery, Problem-Based, Experiential, and Inquiry-Based Teaching' in *Educational Psychologist, Volume 41*, page 84, Lawrence Erlbaum Associates
6. Heath, C. and Heath D. (2010) *Teaching That Sticks*, page 1. Retrieved from http://heathbrothers.com/download/mts-teaching-that-sticks.pdf
7. Ibid. page 2
8. Willingham, D. (2009) *Why Don't Students Like School?*, page 61, San Francisco, CA: Jossey-Bass
9. Ibid. page 13
10. Heath, C. and Heath D. (2010) *Teaching That Sticks*, page 4
11. Young, M. and Lambert, D. with Roberts, C. and Roberts, M. (2015) *Knowledge and the Future School*, pages 10 and 100, London: Bloomsbury
12. Willingham, D. (2009) *Why Don't Students Like School?*, page 90, San Francisco, CA: Jossey-Bass
13. Didau, D. and Rose, N. (2016) *What Every Teacher Needs to Know About . . . Psychology*, page 48, Woodbridge, UK: John Catt
14. Ibid. page 111
15. Didau, D. (2015) *What if Everything You Knew About Education Was Wrong?* page 24, Carmarthen, UK: Crown House
16. Allison, S. and Tharby, A. (2015) *Making Every Lesson Count*, page 69, Carmarthen, UK: Crown House
17. Heath, C. and Heath D. (2010) *Teaching That Sticks*, page 6
18. Tricot, A. and Sweller, J. (2014) *Domain-Specific Knowledge and Why Teaching Generic Skills Does Not Work*, page 9, Toulouse
19. Ibid. page 23
20. Renkl, A. and Atkinson, R. (2003) 'Structuring the Transition From Example Study to Problem Solving in Cognitive Skill Acquisition: A Cognitive Load Perspective' in *Educational Psychologist, Volume 38*, page 17, Lawrence Erlbaum Associates

21. Willingham, D. (2009) *Why Don't Students Like School?*, page 35, San Francisco, CA: Jossey-Bass
22. Heath, C. and Heath D. (2010) *Teaching That Sticks*, page 8
23. Willingham, D. (2009) *Why Don't Students Like School?*, page 66, San Francisco, CA: Jossey-Bass
24. Didau, D. and Rose, N. (2016) *What Every Teacher Needs to Know About . . . Psychology*, page 53, Woodbridge, UK: John Catt
25. Brown, P., Roediger III, H., and McDaniel, M. (2014) *Make it Stick: The Science of Successful Learning*, pages 5 and 76, London: Harvard University Press
26. Willingham, D. (2009) *Why Don't Students Like School?*, pages 90–91, San Francisco, CA: Jossey-Bass
27. Didau, D. and Rose, N. (2016) *What Every Teacher Needs to Know About . . . Psychology*, page 110, Woodbridge, UK: John Catt
28. Rosenshine, B. (2012) 'Principles of Instruction: Research-Based Strategies That All Teachers Should Know' in *American Education*, spring 2012, page 17
29. Ibid. page 14
30. Ibid. page 14
31. Allison, S. and Tharby, A. (2015) *Making Every Lesson Count*, page 79–81, Carmarthen, UK: Crown House
32. Nuthall, G., cited in Hattie, J. (2011) *Visible Learning for Teachers: Maximising Impact on Learning*, page 131, London: Routledge
33. Dunlosky, J., Rawson, K., Marsh, E., Nathan, M., and Willingham, D. (2013) 'Improving Students' Learning with Effective Learning Techniques: Promising Directions from Cognitive and Educational Psychology' in *Psychological Sciences in the Public Interest, Volume 14(1)*, page 8, SAGE publishing
34. Ibid. page 11
35. Brown, P., Roediger III, H., and McDaniel, M. (2014) *Make it Stick: The Science of Successful Learning*, pages 5 and 126, London: Harvard University Press
36. Ibid. page 6
37. Farrington, C., Roderick, M., Allensworth, E., Nagaoka, J., Seneca Keyes, T., Johnson, D., and Beechum, N., (2012) *Teaching Adolescents to Become Learners: The Role of Non-Cognitive Factors in Shaping School Performance, a Critical Literature Review*, page 40, University of Chicago
38. https://evidenceintopractice.wordpress.com/2014/08/25/does-visual-mapping-help-revision/
39. Ibid.
40. Didau, D. (2015) *What if Everything You Knew About Education Was Wrong?* page 180, Carmarthen, UK: Crown House
41. Willingham, D. (2009) *Why Don't Students Like School?*, page 44, San Francisco, CA: Jossey-Bass
42. Brown, P., Roediger III, H., and McDaniel, M. (2014) *Make it Stick: The Science of Successful Learning*, page 75, London: Harvard University Press

43. Didau, D. and Rose, N. (2016) *What Every Teacher Needs to Know About . . . Psychology*, page 47, Woodbridge, UK: John Catt
44. Ibid. page 113
45. Ibid. pages 109–119

Chapter 6

Practising to fluency

The more we practice, the better we perform.
Dan Heath claims that, "Practice doesn't make perfect, practice makes permanent."[1]

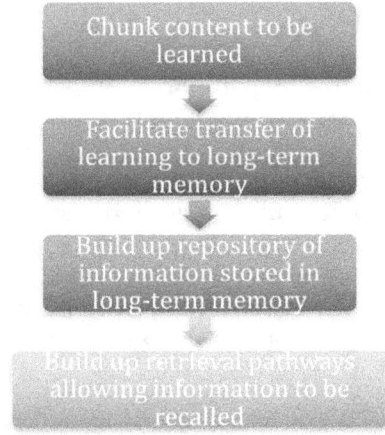

Understanding is not enough. It may be insecure, artificially buoyed up by the clarity of the teacher's explanation, or it may be ephemeral.

How often have you heard students say, "I could do it in the lesson?" It is easy for students to mistake the fluency of the teacher's explanation with their own fluency of understanding and in classroom conditions they can be buoyed up by the cues provided by the teacher.

Fluency in learning, as in sport and music, is achieved when students 'think hard' about what they are learning by practising this until they are fluent. Daniel Willingham suggests that, "it is virtually impossible to become proficient at a mental task without extended practice."[2] Practice also speeds up future learning because "it reduces that amount of 'room' that mental work requires."[3] In *Make it Stick*, Brown et al. explain that increased practice builds greater myelin along the brain's pathways, improving the strength and speed of electrical signals, and therefore performance.[4]

In his research on effective teaching, Rosenshine found that the most successful teachers ensured that students practised both extensively and successfully, both during and after lessons.[5] This practice was more effective for being intertwined with formative assessment in a blend of:

- Guided practice;
- Questioning to check for understanding;
- Correcting of errors; and
- Problem solving.[6]

Rosenshine regards the importance of practice in the learning journey from 'learning' to 'learned' as being the opportunity that it gives for "sufficient rehearsal"[7] in order to prevent forgetting. Explanation without practice would mean that this vital 'rehearsal' of knowledge did not take place. The more a student rehearses their knowledge, the more strongly it is embedded in long-term memory.

In order for new knowledge that has been presented through explanation to be retained in, and retrieved from, long-term memory, students need to interact with it through activities such as:

- Rephrasing;
- Elaborating; and
- Summarising.

> In order to achieve this Rosenshine suggests that practice should include:[8]
>
> - Asking questions that enable students to process and rehearse the knowledge to be learned;
> - Summarising the main points of the knowledge to be learned;

- Supervised practice;
- Activities that allow deep processing of the knowledge to be learned; and
- Feedback.

And extensive practice does mean 'extensive.' It was Ericsson's research on the role of deliberate practice in the acquisition of expert performance[9] that formed the basis for the 10,000 rule featured in Malcolm Gladwell's 2009 book *Outliers*,[10] explaining why some people achieve more than others. In his rather startlingly titled book, *War Against Schools: Academic Child Abuse*, Siegfried Engelmann suggests that "the amount of practice required is five times what teachers expect."[11]

This is another argument against reducing the unit of learning to a lesson, which may confuse students (and parents) as to the timeframe over which learning and practice need to occur.

This chapter considers six aspects of successful practice:

Six aspects of successful practice:

Aspect 1: Successful practice is deliberate

American Doug Lemov, whose book *Teach Like a Champion* was described in 2014 as "Britain's latest teaching bible,"[12] argues (along with the other authors of *Practice Perfect*) that the transformative power of practice has been underestimated: "Generally seen as mundane and humdrum, poorly used and much maligned, or too familiar to be interesting, practice is often considered unworthy of deep, sustained reflection and precise engineering."[13]

We often understand the concept of 'practice' best when applied to 'practical' subjects. For example, we learn how to play the piano through repeated practice. In fact, all subjects are 'practical' in that understanding of knowledge, concepts or technical proficiency requires as much 'rehearsal' in an academic subject as it does in a practical one.

Repetition of a task will eventually make it automatic; however, in *Make it Stick*, Brown *et al.* expose "the fallacy in thinking that repetitive exposure [alone] builds memory."[14] The key is not just practice, but that the practice is thoughtful. This has been termed 'deliberate practice.' Similarly, Doug Lemov *et al.* point out in *Practice Perfect* that, "it's better to do it slow and right than fast and not quite right . . . less practice of better quality could yield more preferable results than more practice of lesser quality."[15]

Deliberate practice to fluency speeds up the future learning process because once learning is automatic it creates more room in working memory.

Aspect 2: Successful practice is focused

It is vital that thinking during practice is focused on that which is to be learned. Daniel Willingham says that "to teach well, you should pay careful attention to what an assignment will actually make students think about (not what you hope they will think about), because that is what they will remember."[16]

In *Making Every Lesson Count*, Allison and Tharby point out that this should include practising micro-detail as well as at macro level: I.e. sentences and short answers as well as essays and exam papers.[17] Similarly, in *Making Good Progress?*, Daisy Christodolou emphasises the importance of the "deliberate-practice method" in which skills are broken down into their component parts: "The best way to develop skills may not always look like the skill itself."[18] This "narrow and focused"[19] practice also prevents working memory becoming overloaded and allows the learner to concentrate on one area of performance.

Doug Lemov et al. regard this as the difference between "drill" focused on skill development, and "scrimmage" focused on evaluation and final preparation.[20]

Aspect 3: Successful practice is effortful

In *Make it Stick* Brown et al. remind us that deliberate practice is not necessarily "enjoyable;"[21] another 'nail in the coffin' of the theory that effective learning is 'fun.' Neither does it necessarily lead to smooth progress. In *Mastery*, George Leonard describes the 'mastery curve':

> Learning any new skill involves relatively brief spurts of progress, each of which is followed by a slight decline to a plateau somewhat higher in most cases than that which preceded it . . . the upward spurts vary; the plateaus have their own dips and rises along the way . . . To take the master's journey, you have to practise diligently, striving to hone your skills, to attain new levels of competence. But while doing so – and this is the inexorable fact of the journey – you also have to be willing to spend most of your time on a plateau, to keep practising even when you seem to be getting nowhere.[22]

Doug Lemov et al. outline the benefits of 'drills,' which "maximise the amount of mental energy focused on a skill. They increase density, the number of productive iterations of a skills per minute of practice . . . through frequent, intentional, close-quarters repetition."[23]

Aspect 4: Successful practice requires knowledge

Just as all subjects are 'practical' in that they require practice, all subjects also require two sets of knowledge:

- Propositional knowledge of facts, sometimes described as knowledge 'of'; and
- Procedural knowledge of processes, sometimes described as knowledge of 'how to'.

The description of 'higher' and 'lower' order skills can be misleading.

Knowledge and understanding are not subordinate 'lower' skills that can be skipped over, but prerequisites to 'higher order' skills that *cannot* exist without them. Bloom's Taxonomy is therefore viewed more helpfully horizontally, rather than vertically, as stages to 'fluency:'

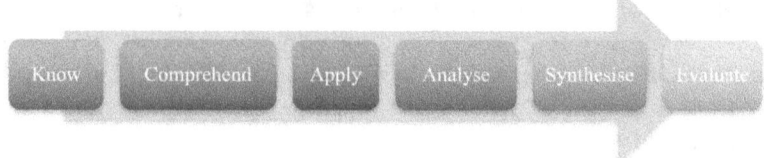

A key word is 'critical' or, if you prefer, 'convincing.' Without knowledge we cannot critically or convincingly analyse or evaluate, and we must ask whether there is any point in uncritical or unconvincing analysis.

In *Critical Thinking*, Daniel Willingham explains that students cannot transfer critical thinking skills from one subject domain to another because "thought processes are intertwined with what is being thought about ... [Therefore] the ability to think critically depends on domain knowledge and practice."[24]

E. D. Hirsch, the 'godfather' of the concept of 'core knowledge' suggests that,

> breadth of knowledge is the single factor within human control that contributes most to academic achievement and general cognitive competence. Breadth of knowledge is a far greater factor in achievement than socio-economic status ... [therefore] imparting broad knowledge to all children is the single most effective way to narrow the gap between demographic groups through schooling.[25]

In *Making Good Progress?*, Daisy Christodolou is keen to stress that,

> generic-skill lessons are not actually effective in instilling the skills they claim to because they misinterpret skill as something that is generic when, in fact, skill is specific ... dependent on large bodies of domain-specific knowledge ... not easily transferable to different domains.[26]

She also emphasises the importance of increasing students' knowledge through teaching of vocabulary, for example the explicit teaching of the Tier Two words that occur regularly in prose, but less regularly in spoken language.[27]

Similarly, Didau and Rose point out that 'far transfer' between different subject domains is "much more difficult than is often supposed."[28]

> Knowledge and understanding are necessary requirements for analysis to occur

> Analysis without knowledge and understanding will not lead to knowledge and understanding and will not be deep or critical

In *Principles of Instruction* Rosenshine finds that the greater and better connected a student's domain knowledge:

- The easier it is for them to acquire new knowledge;
- The easier it is for them to retrieve knowledge;
- The easier it is for them to problem-solve; and
- The more space they have available in working memory.[29]

However, knowledge alone is insufficient. Writer Ferdinand Mount, cited in Martin Robinson's thought-provoking book *Trivium*, points out that is it "impossible for . . . [our knowledge] base to be secure if we have not brought a critical intelligence to bear on the information being thrown at us."[30]

Aspect 5: Successful practice is successful

In *Principles of Instruction,* Rosenshine found that the optimal success rate for fostering student achievement appeared to be about 80 per cent.[31]

This level of success demonstrates that students are learning effectively but are still sufficiently challenged. Rosenshine suggests that learning with a lesser success rate runs the risk of students learning and practising misconceptions that may be difficult to reverse once they have become embedded in students' schemas. This success rate is important for students of all ability.[32]

As Doug Lemov et al. put it in *Practice Perfect*, "practice should involve people practicing [sic] success."[33] Therefore, practice activities should be engineered so that the success rate is "reliably high."[34] They suggest that,

> checking for mastery requires responding to failure to remediate it as quickly and as positively as you can ... If the error is persistent and prevalent, ask yourself whether there needs to be so much of it. Why not redesign the process instead, eliminating complexity or variables to make the task temporarily simpler, breaking a chain of skills down to focus on just one, or slowing things down so there's time to process the complexity.[35]

Didau and Rose also remind us of the link between success and motivation: "Rather than motivation resulting in improved performance, it seems that improved performance leads to increased motivation."[36]

Aspect 6: Successful practice follows the order of learning

Novices and experts learn differently.

Daniel Willingham explains that, "cognition early in training is fundamentally different from cognition late in training."[37] This can be described as one of the 'real' learning styles of learners, and it needs to be taken into account by teachers when planning instructional sequences.

Dylan Wiliam points out that,

> the starkest difference between experts and novices is not so much in the amount of knowledge but in how it is organised ... [In one study] novices tended to group problems according to surface features ... whereas experts grouped problems on the basis of major principles.[38]

In *Principles of Instruction*, Rosenshine suggests that novice learners require scaffolds or **'guided practice'** that can be withdrawn as they become more expert. This process of scaffolding work has been called "cognitive apprenticeship"[39] and is vital before students move onto independent practice.

An understanding of how the memory works suggests the following sequence of 'fading' practice:

1. Guided instruction using worked examples;
2. Problem solving; and
3. Interleaved practice.

In *Why Minimal Guidance During Instruction Does Not Work*, Kirschner *et al.* are clear that when teaching new knowledge, students "should be explicitly shown what to do and how to do it . . . [as novices] learn more deeply from strongly guided learning than from discovery."[40]

The **'worked example effect:'** That novices learn more effectively from studying worked examples than from solving equivalent problems, occurs because problem-solving places a greater load on working memory and is therefore a less effective and efficient way of transferring knowledge to long-term memory. This is because:

- The aim of problem solving is to search for a solution, not to remember knowledge; and
- Therefore working memory is used up on the activity of searching rather than remembering.

In comparison, studying worked examples eliminates the need to search for solutions so that the working memory can concentrate on learning new knowledge.

Rosenshine suggests using a sequence of worked-out examples followed by students working out partially completed problems and finally regular problems.[41] The process of students working from fully worked examples, through a series of partially worked examples in which the 'worked' element gradually reduces, to problems in which there is no worked element is sometimes described as a 'fading procedure.'

> Renkl and Atkinson identify three stages to skills acquisition:[42]
>
> 1. **An early phase** in which learners attempt to gain a basic understanding of the domain. This fits with the 'explanation' phase of instruction.
> 2. **An intermediate phase** in which learners focus on learning how to solve problems. This is the 'practice' phase of instruction in which students' knowledge base should be secure and correct through the correcting of misconceptions.
>
> Renkl and Atkinson suggest that in order for students to learn information effectively they have to "actively self-explain" solutions during this stage of learning in addition to studying examples and problem solving.
>
> 3. **A late stage** in which speed and accuracy are heightened by practice.
>
> Renkl and Atkinson believe that at this late stage students should be focusing on the speed, accuracy and automaticity of problem solving; therefore self-explanations should have become redundant and unnecessary.

Expertise reversal effect

Conversely, the 'worked example effect' reverses as learners gain expertise because experts have the domain knowledge required to solve problems using their long-term memory and, therefore, do not need to drain their working memory with extensive searches. In the case of an expert, providing worked examples is a redundant activity that will actually increase extraneous cognitive load, and their time is better spent practising problem solving to increase automaticity.

For students gaining expertise, problem solving is a more effective type of practice because it involves them generating information.

In *Make it Stick*, Brown *et al.* suggest that searching for a solution and retrieving related knowledge from memory encourages

> deep processing of the answer when it is later supplied ... in a way that simply reading the answer cannot. It's better to solve a problem than to memorise a solution. It's better to attempt a solution and supply the incorrect answer than not to make the attempt.[43]

Students who have spent time attempting to solve a problem will remember the solution more effectively when it is provided.[44]

This expert state is built by hours of practice in varying conditions.

Didau and Rose remind us that "students can learn in one context, yet fail to transfer to other contexts,"[45] always a source of frustration to teachers, which explains why the 'desirable difficulty' of varied practice is needed to embed expertise.

Experts have also practised *to* automaticity. This is very different to being automatically expert. Dylan Wiliam describes automaticity as being one of the "hallmarks of expertise."[46]

Practice that follows the order of learning is more efficient

Learning activities add three types of cognitive load to working memory:

1. The *intrinsic* load of the content. This is a mixture of the inherent difficulty of the content and the prior knowledge of the learner. The greater the prior knowledge of the learner, the less the intrinsic load of the content.
2. The *germane* load of the learning activity. This refers to the cognitive load of the learning activities. As explained above, the germane load can change depending on what stage of learning the activity is being used at.
3. *Extraneous* load. This refers to any mental activities during learning that do not contribute directly to learning. Obviously, the teacher should aim to eliminate extraneous load.

Proponents of Cognitive Load Theory suggest that selecting learning activities that reduce cognitive load improves the capacity of working memory. This might be done through:

- Ensuring greater prior knowledge of learners;
- Ensuring that learning activities are used at the optimum time in the learning sequence; and
- Removing any unnecessary activities.

The order in which practice activities are deployed is important in increasing or reducing cognitive capacity. A 'reversal' or 'redundancy effect' occurs as learners gain expertise, in which activities that were previously valuable become redundant and in fact increase cognitive load.

What activity represents cognitive load depends on the stage of skills acquisition that the learner is at

Table 6.1

Learning Phase	Activity	Cognitive rationale
Early	Gaining basic understanding of the domain through explanation.	This frees the learner from performance demands so that they can concentrate on gaining understanding.
Intermediate	Focusing on how to solve problems through worked examples and self-explanation	Active self-explaining is important in this phase to learn the rationale of how to apply basic knowledge.
Late	Developing speed and accuracy through problem solving.	The aim in this phase is automaticity, therefore self-explana explanations are not helpful and worked examples are redundant.

Renkl and Atkinson[47]

The role of mistakes also changes during the skills acquisition process

As learners are developing their rules for solving problems, instruction that reduces errors, and immediately corrects them, is most appropriate. As problem solving becomes more complex however, errors become a useful part of the learning process because they "trigger reflections and thereby deepen understanding of the domain."[48]

Because learning occurs over time, there are four types of practice that need to be planned for:

Four types of practice

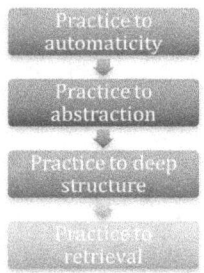

1. Practice to automaticity

Mental processes can become automatic. With propositional knowledge we tend to call this learning 'off by heart.'

Automaticity is arguably even more important for effective procedural knowledge.

Familiar examples are driving a car or tying a shoelace. To gain either propositional or procedural automaticity, fluency and permanency we need to 'overlearn' or 'over-practise' information or processes so that they become deeply embedded. In *Make it Stick*, Brown *et al.* explain that, with sufficient practice, ideas or skills can "fuse" into a "mental model" that could be described as a "brain app."[49]

Once this has been done, there is space in the working memory for new learning to occur.

As Willingham explains, the automaticity of basic skills, such as reading and multiplication tables are crucial in order to:

- Learn more advanced skills;
- Prevent forgetting; and
- Improve transfer of knowledge from one context to another.[50]

David Didau points out that rote learning

> remains a much maligned and neglected method of teaching ... We don't even consider whether rote learning might sometimes be an effective tool; we just know, deep in our hearts, that it's an instrument of evil, born in some bleak Gradgrindian hellhole.[51]

In comparison to the jaundiced view of drilling that Didau conjures up above, Doug Lemov *et al.* quote John Wooden that "Drilling creates a foundation on which individual initiative and imagination can flourish."[52]

2. Practice to abstraction

Given what we know about the abstract nature of culturally constructed secondary knowledge and 'powerful knowledge' it is important that students can abstract learning and apply it to new contexts. Daniel Willingham points out that while knowledge remains tied to analogy it will remain shallow.[53]

3. Practice to deep structure

Key to expertise is the understanding of the deep, rather than surface, structure of problems.

Daniel Willingham explains that "to see the deep structure, you must understand how all parts of the problem relate to one another, and you must know which parts are important and which are not."[54] He points out that this is important because we can pay too much attention to surface structure:

> Inflexible knowledge is meaningful, but narrow; it's narrow in that it is tied to a concept's surface structure and the deep structure of the concept is not easily accessed. 'Deep structure' refers to a principle that transcends specific examples.[55]

This preoccupation with surface structure could be because novices and experts think differently. In *Domain-Specific Knowledge*, Tricot and Sweller explain that while novice learners work backwards from a goal, expert learners work forwards.[56] Novices are more likely to focus on surface features rather than seeing the 'deep structure' and unifying underlying principles.

Daisy Christodolou points out that experts have "rich and detailed structures of knowledge stored in their long-term memory. These structures – often called schema or mental models – are what allow the expert to encounter new problems and solve them with such ease."[57]

Interleaving

Interleaving can help with practice to deep structure. This involves mixing up, or interleaving, multiple similar concepts, problems or processes to encourage students to discriminate between them. It has the following advantages:

- It helps students to distinguish between similar concepts that they find confusing.
- It makes it easier for learners to compare and contrast members of one category or process with members of another, thereby understanding the deep structural differences between them.
- It tests the depth of student understanding more accurately. In a research paper entitled, *Interleaving Helps Students Distinguish Among Similar Concepts*, Rohrer points out that blocking (the opposite process to interleaving) "leads students to believe that they understand material better than they actually do . . . [thereby giving] an illusion of knowing."[58]
- It is a 'desirable difficulty.' By working harder to retrieve and 're-load' information it strengthens retrieval pathways.
- It helps the transfer of knowledge from one context to another.

In *Make it Stick*, Brown *et al.* point out that although interleaved practice feels slower, "research shows unequivocally that mastery and long-term retention are much better if you interleave practice than if you mass it." [59]

4. Practice for retrieval

Fluency alone does not guarantee that knowledge has been effectively learned. That students can do a task in a 'constant' environment of similar, immediate, massed practice with immediate corrective feedback, is not necessarily a predictor that they will be able to do the same task when practice is varied, interleaved, and spaced with delayed corrective feedback.

The second set of conditions form the characteristics for both real life and most examinations. Therefore, as teachers, we need to give students opportunities for practice that prepares them for an inconstant environment.

Graham Nuthall's findings suggested that students retain 80 per cent of information once they have received three re-presentations of it.[60] In *Making Every Lesson Count,* Shaun Allison and Andy Tharby remind us that, sadly, this type of, "careful iterative teaching is not in vogue."[61]

For this reason, practice needs to include 'desirable difficulties.' The 'difficult' recall of learning is more effective because it requires on-going 'reloading' of the knowledge to be learned from long-term memory. As permanent learning requires the 'learning' in the working memory to transfer to the 'learned' in the long-term memory, this use of long-term memory is good.

Examples of 'desirable difficulties' include:

- Varying the conditions of practice rather than keeping them constant and predictable;
- Spacing practice sessions with gaps to allow forgetting;
- Interleaving rather than blocking practice;
- Testing rather than re-studying information; and
- Reducing feedback.

Didau and Rose suggest that,

> whilst there's no benefit in introducing struggle at the point of encoding ... there do appear to be compelling reasons to believe that certain 'desirable difficulties' at the point of retrieval help to increase students' ability to both retain and transfer ... content.[62]

The 'difficult' recall of knowledge both strengthens the interconnections between networks of knowledge and increases the cues for retrieving knowledge.

Spacing

The spacing effect is the finding that "information that is presented repeatedly over spaced intervals is learned much better than information that is repeated without intervals (i.e. massed practice). This effect is one of the most robust results in all of cognitive psychology."[63]

Consequently, in their helpful guide into 'What Works, What Doesn't,' Dunlosky *et al.* identified this 'distributed practice' as one of their "two clear winners" in effective study.[64]

This is because having to recall the information decreases its accessibility; thereby requiring the learner to 'think harder.' With successive spaced practices, knowledge is learned better, and forgotten more slowly.

In a research paper entitled *Using Spacing to Enhance Diverse Forms of Learning*, Carpenter *et al.* outline:

- The 'spacing effect:' Studying information across two or more spaced sessions "often produces better learning than spending the same amount of time studying the material in a single session."[65]
- The 'lag effect:' Different spacing gaps result in different levels of learning. The optimal spacing gap was 10–20 per cent of the test delay (i.e. a 1–2 week spacing if the test is 10 weeks away), although "research suggests that expanding schedules might be better for short-term retention, and fixed schedules might be better for longer-term retention."[66]

The disadvantage of massed practice (the opposite of spacing) is that it can give rise to the 'illusion of fluency,' in which temporary familiarity is mistaken for permanent mastery.

In comparison, spacing "arrests forgetting"[67] because it involves the spaced 'reloading' of the knowledge to be learned from long-term memory, which helps to consolidate the learning.

Fifteen questions for the professional practitioner to ask

Table 6.2

Question	Action
1. How do I ensure that my students undertake extensive, successful practice?	
2. How do I ensure that my students practice both micro-detail and macro level work?	
3. How do I ensure 80% success rates in practice? For all?	
4. How do I ensure that I respond quickly to misconceptions in the guided practice stage?	
5. How does my practice follow the stages of learning?	
6. How do I use 'fading' practice: Worked examples, partially worked examples, problem solving, interleaved problems?	

continued

Table 6.2 continued

Question	Action
7. How do I use scaffolds, worked examples and guided practice?	_____
8. How do I withdraw these as students gain expertise?	_____
9. How do I use problem solving that builds speed and accuracy?	_____
10. How do I develop students' automaticity?	_____
11. How do I move students from concrete to abstract practice?	_____
12. How do I ensure that students have 'deep structure' understanding?	_____
13. How do I use interleaving?	_____
14. How do I use spacing?	_____
15. How do I use varied practice?	_____

Fifteen ways to save time with practising to fluency

Save learning time

1. Build more time for distributed practice into your medium term curriculum sequences to speed up later learning.
2. Use homework for independent practice so that you can maximise the time spent on this.
3. Don't waste time on ineffective types of practice. Some types of practice are not as helpful to retrieval as others. In *Improving Students' Learning with Effective Learning Techniques: Promising Directions from Cognitive and Educational Psychology*,[68] Dunlosky *et al.* find testing, distributed practice and student self-explanation to be more effective than summarising, highlighting and re-reading information.
4. Save working memory and build student expertise by engaging in 'narrow' practice and drilling of the component parts of learning.
5. Save working memory time by building more teaching to automaticity into your practice so that students are automatic and fluent in the basic building blocks of learning.

6. Make practice quicker and more effective by moving through a 'fading' procedure from worked examples, through guided practice to independent practice.
7. Whatever stage of practice a student is at, move the practice on once they reach an 80 per cent success rate.

Save learning time by reducing students' cognitive load

8. Reduce the intrinsic load of learning activities by building up students' background knowledge over time.
9. Save time later and reduce cognitive load by explicitly teaching vocabulary, in particular, Tier 2 words.
10. Reduce extraneous cognitive load: Don't waste time on 'discovery' learning or initial problem solving. Start the learning process with clear teacher explanation and modelling using scaffolds/ worked examples.
11. Reduce extraneous cognitive load and 'redundant' activities: Don't waste time on scaffolds or self-explanation once students have gained expertise.

Save time on resources

12. Use more teacher explanation, worked examples/models, student self-explanation and problem solving.
13. Don't be afraid to use textbooks to find the above.

Save time on written feedback

14. During the initial stage of learning, feedback should be immediate; therefore use 'live' marking.
15. During the late stage of learning, feedback should be delayed; therefore cut back on excessive teacher guidance.

Where does practice fit in the instruction sequence?

Practice needs to occur after initial explanation, but should then form part of a fluid sequence of:

- Guided practice;
- Questioning to check for understanding;
- Correcting of errors through more immediate feedback;

- Moving in a 'fading process' from carefully guided practice to fully independent practice;
- On going questioning to check for understanding; and
- On going correcting of errors though increasingly delayed feedback.

Notes

1. Heath, D., cited in Lemov, D., Woolway, E. and Yezzi, K. (2012) *Practice Perfect: 42 Rules for Getting Better and Better*, page xii, San Francisco, CA: Jossey Bass
2. Willingham, D. (2009) *Why Don't Students Like School?*, page 107, San Francisco, CA: Jossey-Bass
3. Ibid.
4. Brown, P., Roediger III, H., and McDaniel, M. (2014) *Make it Stick: The Science of Successful Learning*, page 171, London: Harvard University Press
5. Rosenshine, B. (2012) 'Principles of Instruction: Research-Based Strategies That All Teachers Should Know' in *American Education, spring 2012*, page 19
6. Ibid. page 17
7. Ibid. page 16
8. Ibid. page 16
9. Ericsson, K., Krampe, R. and Tesch-Romer, C. (1993) 'The Role of Deliberate Practice in the Acquisition of Expert Performance' in *Psychological Review, Volume 100*, pages 363–403
10. Gladwell, M. (2009) *Outliers: The Story of Success*, London: Penguin
11. Engelmann, S. (1992) *War Against Schools: Academic Child Abuse*, page 17, Portland, OR: Halcyon House
12. www.theguardian.com/education/2014/oct/12/american-wrote-classroom-bible-doug-lemov
13. Lemov, D., Woolway, E. and Yezzi, K. (2012) *Practice Perfect: 42 Rules for Getting Better and Better*, page xvii, San Francisco, CA: Jossey Bass
14. Brown, P., Roediger III, H., and McDaniel, M. (2014) *Make it Stick: The Science of Successful Learning*, page 13, London: Harvard University Press
15. Lemov, D., Woolway, E. and Yezzi, K. (2012) *Practice Perfect: 42 Rules For Getting Better And Better*, pages 3 and 23, San Francisco, CA: Jossey Bass
16. Ibid. page 54
17. Allison, S. and Tharby, A. (2015) *Making Every Lesson Count*, page 142–143, Carmarthen, UK: Crown House
18. Christodolou, D. (2016) *Making Good Progress? The Future of Assessment for Learning*, page 23, Oxford: Oxford University Press
19. Ibid. page 41
20. Lemov, D., Woolway, E. and Yezzi, K. (2012) *Practice Perfect: 42 Rules for Getting Better and Better*, page 50, San Francisco, CA: Jossey Bass

21. Brown, P., Roediger III, H., and McDaniel, M. (2014) *Make it Stick: The Science of Successful Learning*, page 184, London: Harvard University Press
22. Leonard, G. (1992) *Mastery: The Keys to Success and Long-Term Fulfilment*, pages 14–15, New York: Plume
23. Lemov, D., Woolway, E. and Yezzi, K. (2012) *Practice Perfect: 42 Rules for Getting Better and Better*, page 49, San Francisco, CA: Jossey Bass
24. Willingham, D. (2007) 'Critical Thinking: Why Is It So Hard to Teach?' in *American Educator*, pages 8 and 17
25. Hirsch, E. (2006) *The Knowledge Deficit: Closing the Shocking Education Gap for American Children*, page 106
26. Christodolou, D. (2016) *Making Good Progress? The Future of Assessment for Learning*, page 33, Oxford: Oxford University Press
27. Ibid. page 153
28. Didau, D. and Rose, N. (2016) *What Every Teacher Needs to Know About . . . Psychology*, page 63, Woodbridge, UK: John Catt
29. Ibid. page 19
30. Robinson, M. (2013) *Trivium 21c: Preparing Young People for the Future with Lessons from the Past*, page 183, Carmarthen, UK: Crown House
31. Rosenshine, B. (2012) 'Principles of Instruction: Research-Based Strategies That All Teachers Should Know' in *American Education*, spring 2012, page 17
32. Ibid. pages 17 and 21
33. Lemov, D., Woolway, E. and Yezzi, K. (2012) *Practice Perfect: 42 Rules for Getting Better and Better*, page 11, San Francisco, CA: Jossey Bass
34. Ibid. page 28
35. Ibid. pages 26 and 28
36. Didau, D. and Rose, N. (2016) *What Every Teacher Needs To Know About . . . Psychology*, page 168, Woodbridge, UK: John Catt
37. Willingham, D. (2009) *Why Don't Students Like School?*, page 127, San Francisco, CA: Jossey-Bass
38. Wiliam, D. (2016) *Leadership [For] Teaching Learning: Creating a Culture Where All Teachers Improve so That All Students Succeed*, page 144, West Palm Beach, FL: Learning Sciences International
39. Rosenshine, B. (2012) 'Principles of Instruction: Research-Based Strategies That All Teachers Should Know' in *American Education*, spring 2012, page 18
40. Kirschner, P., Sweller, J. and Clark, R. (2006) 'Why Minimal Guidance During Instruction Does Not Work: An Analysis of the Failure of Constructivist, Discovery, Problem-Based, Experiential, and Inquiry-Based Teaching' in *Educational Psychologist, Volume 41*, page 79, Lawrence Erlbaum Associates
41. Rosenshine, B. (2012) 'Principles of Instruction: Research-Based Strategies That All Teachers Should Know' in *American Education*, spring 2012, page 15
42. Renkl, A. and Atkinson, R. (2003) 'Structuring the Transition From Example Study to Problem Solving in Cognitive Skill Acquisition: A

Cognitive Load Perspective' in *Educational Psychologist, Volume 38*, page 16, Lawrence Erlbaum Associates
43. Brown, P., Roediger III, H., and McDaniel, M. (2014) *Make it Stick: The Science of Successful Learning*, page 88, London: Harvard University Press
44. Ibid. page 86
45. Didau, D. and Rose, N. (2016) *What Every Teacher Needs to Know About . . . Psychology*, page 63, Woodbridge, UK: John Catt
46. Wiliam, D. (2016) *Leadership [For] Teaching Learning: Creating a Culture Where All Teachers Improve so That All Students Succeed*, page 146, West Palm Beach, FL: Learning Sciences International
47. Renkl, A. and Atkinson, R. (2003) 'Structuring the Transition From Example Study to Problem Solving in Cognitive Skill Acquisition: A Cognitive Load Perspective' in *Educational Psychologist, Volume 38*, Lawrence Erlbaum Associates
48. Ibid. page 19
49. Brown, P., Roediger III, H., and McDaniel, M. (2014) *Make it Stick: The Science of Successful Learning*, page 83, London: Harvard University Press
50. Willingham, D. (2009) *Why Don't Students Like School?*, page 108, San Francisco, CA: Jossey-Bass
51. Didau, D. (2015) *What if Everything You Knew About Education Was Wrong?* page 182, Carmarthen, UK: Crown House
52. Lemov, D., Woolway, E. and Yezzi, K. (2012) *Practice Perfect: 42 Rules for Getting Better and Better*, page 36, San Francisco, CA: Jossey Bass
53. Willingham, D. (2009) *Why Don't Students Like School?*, page 94, San Francisco, CA: Jossey-Bass
54. Ibid. page 100
55. Willingham, D. (2002) 'Inflexible Knowledge: The First Step to Expertise' in *American Educator, Volume 26*, page 32
56. Tricot, A. and Sweller, J. (2014) *Domain-Specific Knowledge and Why Teaching Generic Skills Does Not Work*, page 22, Toulouse
57. Christodolou, D. (2016) *Making Good Progress? The Future of Assessment for Learning*, page 34, Oxford: Oxford University Press
58. Rohrer, D. (2012) 'Interleaving Helps Students Distinguish Among Similar Concepts' in *Education Psychology Review, Volume 24*, page 365
59. Brown, P., Roediger III, H., and McDaniel, M. (2014) *Make it Stick: The Science of Successful Learning*, page 51, London: Harvard University Press
60. Nuthall, G. (2007) *The Hidden Lives of Learners*, pages 80–81, Wellington, NZ: New Zealand Council for Educational Research press
61. Allison, S. and Tharby, A. (2015) *Making Every Lesson Count*, page 131, Carmarthen, UK: Crown House
62. Didau, D. and Rose, N. (2016) *What Every Teacher Needs To Know About. . . Psychology*, page 66, Woodbridge, UK: John Catt
63. https://bjorklab.psych.ucla.edu/research/#spacing

64. Dunlosky, J., Rawson, K., Marsh, E., Mitchell, J. and Willingham, D. (2013) 'What Works, What Doesn't' in *Scientific American Mind*, *Volume 24*, page 48
65. Carpenter, S., Cepeda, N., Rohrer, D., Kang, S. and Pashler, H. (2012) 'Using Spacing to Enhance Diverse Forms of Learning: Review of Recent Research and Implications for Instruction' in *Education Psychology Review*, *Volume 24*, page 370
66. Ibid. pages 370 and 374
67. Brown, P., Roediger III, H., and McDaniel, M. (2014) *Make it Stick: The Science of Successful Learning*, page 4, London: Harvard University Press (2014)
68. Dunlosky, J., Rawson, K., Marsh, E., Nathan, M., and Willingham, D. (2013) 'Improving Students' Learning with Effective Learning Techniques: Promising Directions from Cognitive and Educational Psychology' in *Psychological Sciences in the Public Interest*, *Volume 14(1)*, pages 1–58, SAGE publishing

Chapter 7

Questioning as assessment

Learning is invisible.
We don't easily see students thinking hard – although funnily enough we can often spot it when they're not thinking hard! And even if they appear to be thinking hard, we can't necessarily tell that they are thinking hard about the point of the lesson (and neither can they); therefore we need ways when teaching of making learning as visible as possible, to both ourselves and our students, because it is only when learning is visible in some way that we can assess it.

Questions to ask of learning:

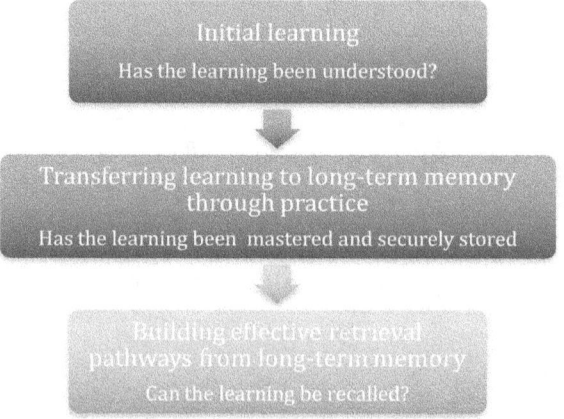

Questioning allows us to clarify and probe, and therefore assess the quality of the learning that has taken place, and (just as importantly) that it has been retained and that it can be retrieved. This questioning might be:

- Written or oral;
- Immediate or delayed;
- Open or closed;
- Deep or shallow; and
- Formal or informal.

And, as Allison and Tharby state in *Making Every Lesson Count*, it should be "ubiquitous and fluid."[1] Once again, they provide an excellent range of strategies in their chapter on questioning.[2]

The quality of the questioning that occurs in teaching, both oral and written, is essential to effective learning.

This chapter hopes to demonstrate that questioning should be a carefully planned process involving informed pedagogical judgement so that the right questions are asked in the right way, at the right time, to ensure an effective 'learning' to 'learned' process.

Sometimes 'questioning as assessment' is divided into three areas: Questioning, assessment and progress checking. I see no reason to make this separation. We progress check through our assessments of students' learning, and we assess through questioning.

There was a vogue a few years ago for 'progress checking' done through use of traffic light colours, lollipop sticks and the like. The problems with this were threefold:

- Students might deliberately give inaccurate feedback – to fit in with everyone else for example;
- Students might accidentally give inaccurate feedback – familiarity, teacher cues and the fluency of the teacher's explanation can give rise to an 'illusion of fluency' so that the student thinks that they understand something whereas in fact their understanding is not secure; and
- Given that the student is a novice rather than an expert how will they 'know that they know' or 'know what they need to know to know that they know'?

Is all assessment formative?

I have written in Chapter 3 about the danger of over-compartmentalising teaching into separate categories of planning, teaching and assessing. The learning process is a fluid one. A wide range of assessing questions should be interwoven into the instruction sequence in order to provide the spectrum of assessment of learning, from the highly informal formative assessment gained from observing students' facial expressions, through to the formal synoptic exam paper.

Given our increasing understanding of 'test-potentiated' learning: That "tests can be valuable learning events"[3] (explored in the next chapter), it could be said that all assessment is formative. Nevertheless, there are good reasons for continuing to think in terms of formative and summative assessment.

Dylan Wiliam provides a helpful explanation that an assessment can be defined as formative or summative based on the inference to be drawn from it:

- Summative: Related to an assessment of the current or future performance of the student; and
- Formative: Related to the planning of future teaching activities[4]

Therefore, a mock exam paper may have a summative and formative function. In *Making Good Progress?*, her book on the future of assessment for learning, Daisy Christodolou argues that it is also vital that summative assessment has some "shared meaning."[5]

Is formative assessment helpful?

In his chapter on formative assessment in *What if Everything You Know About Education Was Wrong?*,[6] David Didau suggests that "Dylan Wiliam's 'big idea' of formative assessment ... might be holed under the waterline"[7] because learning, as opposed to performance, cannot be seen in the present, only in the future. However, if learning does occur in the stages outlined below, then part of the learning process *does* occur in the lesson, and it is this part of the learning process that can be assessed. Therefore, the right caveat is not that formative assessment in the lesson is not "meaningful,"[8] but that formative assessment in the lesson is not 'complete' because it can only assess the initial part of the learning process. Didau argues that correct answers at this stage tell us very little and may indicate mere mimicry of complex concepts;[9] however, as most teachers would agree:

- Any aspect of student understanding is always to be welcomed; and
- Complex concepts are built upon step-by-step explanation, the understanding of which can be meaningfully assessed 'on the spot.'

To state too emphatically that nothing can be known from assessment runs the risk of introducing a 'theoretical Platonism' into teaching that is not helpful to teachers or students.

Dylan Wiliam puts it simply in *Leadership [For] Teacher Learning*: "[Because] students do not necessarily – or even generally – learn exactly what they are taught . . . to be effective, teachers have to find out what their students did actually learn before moving on."[10] If teaching is a process of 'thinking' (pedagogical decision-making) as much as 'doing' then this decision-making must be based on something, and that something should be formative assessment of what is occurring in the classroom. If there is no formative assessment then our teaching is not only not responsive, but it is arguably 'delivery' rather than 'teaching.'

In *Making Good Progress?*, Daisy Christodolou suggests that formative assessment should be:

- Specific: She particularly recommends multiple-choice questions, if carefully constructed using pedagogical content knowledge, as providing precisely targeted specificity that enables the teacher to assess the level of a students' understanding.
- Frequent: Thereby taking advantage of the testing-effect which is explained in Chapter 8: Christodolou describes this as a "powerful argument"[11] for increasing formative assessment.
- Repetitive: In order to ensure the progression from 'learning' to 'learned.'
- Recorded as raw marks. Christodolou suggests that to indicate mastery of an area students should be expected to achieve 90–100 per cent in formatively assessed tasks.[12]

Open and closed questions can be used

Closed questions are often seen as inferior to open questions; however, as Allison and Tharby explain, "Before we move students on to open questions, we need to know if they have got the necessary surface knowledge. This is when closed questions are so important."[13]

Multiple-choice questions can be used

As explained above, carefully crafted multiple-choice questions have the benefit of:

- Accurately assessing student understanding and misunderstanding; and
- Providing a method of assessment that is quick to use (once designed) and reliable to assess.

Thoughtfully constructed multiple-choice questions can be used to diagnose specific subject misconceptions that the teacher is aware of from his or her pedagogical content knowledge. It is also worth considering that multiple-choice questions in which the student has to choose how many of the statements are false or true add another element to their diagnostic potential, as does increasing the number of alternatives given to eliminate lucky guesses. Daisy Christodolou points out that analysing multiple-choice responses also provides the teacher with valuable formative information.[14]

However, when considering the suitability of multiple-choice questions as *summative* rather than formative assessment, it may be worth examining the findings, outlined in Chapter 8, of Brown et al., that generative testing is more effective than 'recognition' testing,[15] and of Endres and Renkl, that learning is most effective when free recall testing is used.[16]

Verbal assessment can be used

Robin Alexander argues that talk is "essential to children's thinking and learning." He points out that "the function of talk in classrooms is cognitive and cultural as well as social."[17] Assessing students' ability to accurately verbalise their understanding is therefore valid.

In *The Secret of Literacy*, David Didau decries the:

> Squeamishness endemic in our education system. Teachers pussy-foot around pupils' inability to articulate clearly or precisely in academic language.[18]

In fact, verbal assessment has the following advantages:

- It allows us to utilise the self-explanation strategies explained in Chapter 5;
- It develops students' use of appropriate academic register in their speech;
- It provides immediate 'live' assessment in the classroom to prevent the embedding of any errors or misconceptions;
- It is quick; and
- It allows immediate, specific and powerful teacher feedback which, being verbal, is also quick and 'live.'

What's not to like?

What about peer and self-assessment?

Given the complex judgements involved in assessing learning, I am not a great advocate of turning assessment into a student 'cottage industry,' particularly as this is often done to reduce teacher workload rather than because it is the most effective form of assessment available. Therefore, my suggestion would be, in the context of this chapter, that if peer assessment is the most effective and efficient form of assessment, and if the form of peer or self-assessment selected is within the realms of students' competence (which is more likely to be the case in assessing simple tasks than complex processes), then it should be used. I do however agree with Daisy Christodolou's verdict that "self-assessing and peer-assessing complex tasks is not straightforward."[19]

Assessment of Learning

Learning occurs in stages and across time, therefore it is important that the process of assessment reflects this. Each stage of learning requires different types of questioning and assessment.

The six stages of assessment linked to the learning process

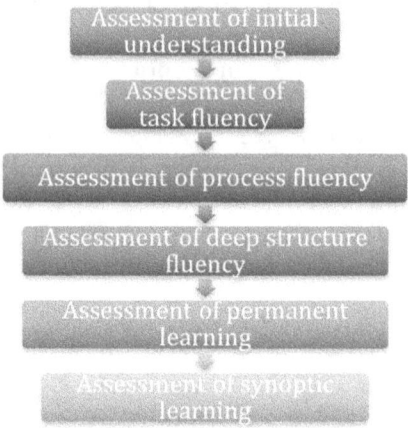

Assessment of initial understanding

Do the students 'get it.' This is the first fundamental and necessary step in learning.

In *Principles of Instruction*, Rosenshine points out the crucial role of questioning in checking for understanding. He found that the most effective teachers asked many more questions, including plenty of process questions, than the least effective teachers.[20]

Dylan Wiliam explains that 'hinge' questions, by which the teacher assesses current student learning in order to make a decision about what action to take next, are a good example of "interactive regulation, in which teachers use formative assessment in real time to make adjustments to their instruction during the act of instruction."[21]

Allison and Tharby suggest that a good 'hinge' question is:

- Simple for the teacher to ask;
- Simple for the students to answer;
- Constructed to assess whether students have grasped/not grasped the salient feature of the learning; and
- Constructed to assess what misconceptions students have acquired.[22]

And questioning should be of all students.

It can be too easy to ask questions to unrepresentative samples of the class: The best students, the worst students, the students with their hands up, the students without their hands up, the students at the front, the students making eye contact with the teacher, the students not making eye contact with the teacher, the students who we think will know the answer, the students who we think will not know the answer.

The most powerful questioning occurs when the understanding of all students is checked simultaneously. However this is done it means that no student can 'hide' and the teacher receives live, immediate and powerful feedback on the students' learning. Framing the right sort of questions to elicit this feedback is an important skill, and developing the right strategies to 'capture' this 100 per cent student response effectively is also vital.

Dylan Wiliam regards teachers' expertise when it comes to checking for understanding as being "relatively underdeveloped," with pedagogical decision-making often based on evidence that is "not representative of the group as a whole." He therefore concludes that this area provides "some of the lowest-hanging fruit" in making teaching more effective.[23]

Assessment of task fluency

Can the students 'do it'?

That a student 'gets' something doesn't necessarily mean that they can do it, or that they can do it correctly, or that they can do it repeatedly, or that they can do it in varied conditions, or that they can do it independently without teacher cues. All of these elements of task fluency need to be assessed.

In *Making Good Progress?*, Daisy Christodolou argues that because skill-acquisition is different to the skill itself, initial assessment should also be very different.[24] For example, in order to develop the complex skill of writing an essay, a series of simple skills and a foundation of knowledge need to be taught – what Christodolou describes as the "hidden body of knowledge."[25] Christodolou derives an analogy from the strength and conditioning exercises that a marathon runner does to improve their performance.[26] This highly task-specific practice also has the advantage of not overloading students' working memories. The assessment of how well these simple skills/materials have been grasped may look very different to the final summative assessment of the essay. Christodolou points out the alternative to this model:

> If every lesson is set up to allow students to demonstrate fully what they are capable of, then lessons start to look less like lessons and more like exams.[27]

Similarly, Daniel Koretz highlights the importance of assessment at this 'micro-level' suggesting that, "if one breaks skills and knowledge into small pieces, one can more easily ascertain which specific skills contribute to a students' weaknesses."[28] This also allows the teacher to assess the impact of other factors that may be impacting on a students' performance. For example, the literacy level of a student will impact on their ability to engage successfully with maths problems even if their understanding of maths is fundamentally sound. This is one of the explanations of the different performance internationally between the TIMSS tests that assess formal mathematical knowledge, and the PISA tests that assess mathematical literacy.

As a useful practical guide, in *Principles of Instruction*, Rosenshine suggests that a success rate of 80 per cent balances effective learning and challenge.[29] Therefore in any assessment of whether a student has acquired effective learning, this figure may be worth bearing in mind.

Assessment of process fluency

Can the students 'do all of it'?

Much of what we ask students to do consists of complex rather than simple knowledge. Writing an essay for example is not merely one simple 'task' but involves a student being able to master all the component parts of the 'process;' therefore the questions above can be asked again when it comes to process. Can the student do every part of the process correctly, in the right sequence, repeatedly, in varied conditions and independently without teacher cues?

In *Promoting Deep Learning Through Teaching and Assessment*, Entwistle found that "assessment which encourages students to think for themselves – such as essay questions, applications to new contexts, and problem-based questions – shifts students . . . towards a deep [learning] approach."[30]

Assessment of deep, rather than surface, structure fluency

Can the students 'do it' in the abstract?

That a student can do something fluently, correctly, repeatedly and independently in varied conditions does not necessarily mean that they understand it in abstraction, or that they understand the deep principles that underlie the superficial surface structure. Without this abstract understanding, or understanding of deep structure, students will not be able to transfer their knowledge to other contexts and therefore 'do it' out of context. It is this level of learning that tends to separate those students whose 'learning' is essentially shallow mimicry, from those who have a deeper understanding.

In *Why Don't Students Like School?* Daniel Willingham points out that, "to see the deep structure, you must understand how all parts of the problem relate to one another, and you must know which parts are important and which parts are not."[31]

Assessment of permanent learning

How much do students get wrong because they don't know, and how much do they get wrong because they once knew but don't any more?

That a student can do every part of a process fluently, correctly, repeatedly and independently in varied conditions, does not necessarily mean that they will be able to do it the next day, week, month, year or decade, although, once they have grasped the deep structure underlying learning, it is likely that their learning will be more permanent.

Very little, if anything, can be 'learned' in its entirety in the unit of a lesson. What is vital is that the learning is stored in long-term memory and can be retrieved from this in the future; an assessment of the 'learned' can therefore only take place after the 'learning' has occurred.

As Nuthall points out "As learning occurs, so does forgetting."[32] We also have the tendency to think that once we 'know' something we will always 'know' it. This can be an illusion; therefore, the only way to 'know what we know' is by assessment at this later stage of the 'learning' to 'learned' process.

Assessment of synoptic learning

Can the students 'do it' when interleaved with other tasks? Massed practice can give rise to the 'illusion of fluency.' To ensure that learning is secure students need to be able to predictably apply it in circumstances that are:

- Varied;
- Delayed; and
- Interleaved across a sufficiently broad sample of the subject domain.

To support this, Chapter 8 outlines the findings of Endres and Renkl that testing may be best if the tests used in the practice phase are the same as the final assessment.[33]

However, Daisy Christodolou warns in *Making Good Progress?* that exam-based assessments (which are by their nature synoptic) can be difficult to use for formative purposes because:

- A summative examination merely samples from the subject domain rather than covering all of it.
- The complexity of many exam questions makes it hard to make accurate diagnostic formative inferences.
- Grading systems for summative exams are intended to measure big subject domains and are therefore not sufficiently sensitive to provide reliable formative feedback on smaller domains. For this reason Christodolou suggests that summative assessment is graded just once or twice a year.[34]

As Christodolou points out, "in plenty of . . .[examiners'] reports, the chief examiners themselves concede that they are not able to work out exactly why pupils struggled with certain questions."[35] She concludes that, "the more complex the task, the less useful it is formatively."[36]

She advises against overly prescriptive rubrics when assessing work and highlights the "great promise" of comparative judgement assessing which "offers the significant gain of being able to grade essays more reliably and quickly than previously . . . [and] refocus classroom practice away from the rubric and towards more helpful analyses of quality".[37]

Key features of an effective assessment

The writing of effective assessments is a highly specialised field. This chapter simply attempts to explain enough for teachers to grasp some of its complexities and to therefore 'know what they don't know' when it comes to assessment writing.

In *What Every Teacher Needs to Know About ... Psychology*, Didau and Rose outline the need for assessments to have:

- Content validity: The assessment contains a representative sample of the knowledge domain;
- Predictive validity: The assessment can be used to predict future performance;
- Reliability: The assessment has been consistently undertaken and assessed;
- Precision: The assessment is a suitably precise measure of student performance; and
- Accuracy: The assessment is a suitably accurate measure of student performance, i.e., not too easy or hard and producing an appropriate range of results that distinguish students from each other.[38]

As they explain, these different elements of an assessment have "trade-off limitations."[39] Closed questions might be more reliable to assess but have less predictive validity in preparation for a History exam, for example.

In *Measuring Up*, a book intended to demystify educational testing, Daniel Koretz, suggests that, "validity is the single most important criterion for evaluating achievement testing."[40]

Daisy Christodolou offers another framework in which assessment can be considered:

- The quality model: Requiring more subjective judgement of the assessment product and therefore risking reliability, for example an essay; and
- The difficulty model: Requiring the construction of appropriate assessment questions and therefore risking validity and accuracy, for example a maths exam. As she points out it can be "extremely hard ... to predict the relative difficulty of different questions."[41]

Labelling from assessment

We like to label in education, and our students like to be labelled – if the label is a positive one for them – and we are, of course, at the mercy of Ofsted who engage in labelling *par excellence*.

Daisy Christodolou suggests that, "even if we did not mean the assessment to be a summative one, the moment we use a grade, a level, or a value-laden statement or word, we are making a summative inference" which may be unreliable.[42]

In *Making Good Progress?*, which is well worth reading for its clear exposition on the purposes of formative and summative assessment, she warns teachers against the Scylla of descriptor-based assessment and the Charybdis of exam-based assessment which she believes lead to:

- Misuse of assessment;
- Over-grading and testing;
- Ineffective feedback;
- Misuse of summative grades; and
- Focus on short-term performance at the expense of long-term learning.[43]

In Chapter 4 of *Making Good Progress?*,[44] Christodolou is highly critical of the formative use of assessment descriptors as:

- Involving judgements around prose descriptors that are likely to be unreliable;
- Involving assessment in lesson which is likely to therefore be inconsistently implemented; and
- Involving teacher judgement that will be subject to biases.[45]

Her critique of too frequent exam-based assessment and grading is that it might, "incentivise ... superficial teaching approaches"[46] if teachers or schools prioritise short-term progress and the narrow instrumentalism of 'teaching to the next test' over long-term learning.

So, to return to education's fixation with labelling, there is also a dissonance between Rosenshine's finding that a success rate of 80 per cent balances effective learning and challenge, and our desire to label learning accurately.[47]

From a cognitive point of view, this is easy to reconcile. The 80 per cent guide is useful in formative assessment of how successful a stage of the learning process has been.

From a psychosocial point of view, this is less easy to reconcile and perhaps points to less frequent summative assessment. If a student is constantly gaining low grades, or 'emerging,' like some reptilian swamp dweller, then they are not experiencing the successful learning that Doug Lemov *et al.* advocate in *Practice Perfect*.[48] Research by McInerney *et al.* into students' academic self-concept found a "reciprocal relationship between academic self-concept and academic achievement,"[49] which is worth considering in the way that we grade and label students.

Table 7.1

Assessment	Examples of this type of assessment	Danger of not assessing it
Of initial understanding	Hinge questions Written or oral	How do you know that students have 'got' it?
Of task fluency	Short practice questions Written or oral	Errors and misconceptions may be picked up which will then be difficult for students to 'unlearn'.
Of process fluency	Long practice questions Written	Students may not be secure at applying learning.
Of deep structure	Interleaved process questions Written	Students may not be able to apply learning to new contexts.
Of permanent learning	Regular, spaced, generative retrieval quizzes	Students may not be able to recall learning.
Of synoptic learning	Interleaved questions All types	Students may not be able to apply learning in a 'real life' or exam setting.

Ten questions for the professional practitioner to ask

Table 7.2

Question	Action
1. How do I use formative assessment?	
2. How do I use summative assessment?	
3. How do I use open and closed questions?	
4. How do I use multiple-choice questions to test for common misconceptions?	
5. How do I use verbal assessment?	
6. How do I ensure that peer assessment is within the competence range of the students?	
7. How do I assess learning across the 6 stages of learning?	
8. How do I construct assessments that are valid, reliable, precise and accurate?	
9. How do I avoid 'teaching to the test'?	
10. How do I prevent over grading?	

Fifteen ways to save time with practising to fluency

Time saving tips when questioning as assessment

Table 7.3

Assessment	Manageable Assessment
Of initial understanding	1. Save time by asking 'live' oral hinge questions in the lesson.
Of task fluency	2. Save time by using: Short practice questions Long practice questions Interleaved process questions From the text book and exam papers rather than designing your own.
Of process fluency	
Of deep structure	
Of permanent learning	3. Save revision and recap time at the end of the course by setting students regular, spaced, generative retrieval quizzes.

1. Save time by using more 'live' verbal questioning and assessment methods in the classroom, rather than written questions and assessment.
2. Save time by creating a bank of multiple-choice questions to assess for common misconceptions.
3. Save time in the learning process by using effective hinge questions to assess where you need to speed up, slow down or change direction.
4. Save time by using 100 per cent questioning methods to assess the understanding of all students at the same time.
5. Reduce the pressure on students' working memories by assessing the components of a process, not just the full process.
6. Save time by reducing the number of summative assessments to one or two a year.
7. Save moderation time by focusing more assessment on student mastery of knowledge and skills that can be more quickly and easily marked.
8. Save time by assessing the 'quality model' using comparative judgement.
9. Save time by leaving summative assessment construction to the experts rather than spending time creating assessments that may not by particularly good.
10. Save time by not over-grading using assessment descriptors and exam-based assessment.
11. Save time by investing in national assessment products.
12. Save time by keeping it simple – students working to 80 per cent plus in formative assessment in order to demonstrate mastery.

Where does assessment fit in the instruction sequence?

As outlined in the chapter above, assessment occurs across the stages of learning:

- Assessment of initial understanding;
- Assessment of task fluency;
- Assessment of process fluency;
- Assessment of deep structure fluency;
- Assessment of permanent learning; and
- Assessment of synoptic learning.

Notes

1. Allison, S. and Tharby, A. (2015) *Making Every Lesson Count*, page 202, Carmarthen, UK: Crown House
2. Ibid. pages 201–237
3. Richland, L., Kornell, N. and Kao, L. (2009) 'The Pre-Testing Effect: Do Unsuccessful Retrieval Attempts Enhance Learning?' in *Journal of Experimental Psychology: Applied*, Volume 15, page 254
4. Wiliam, D. (2016) *Leadership [For] Teaching Learning: Creating a Culture Where All Teachers Improve so that All Students Succeed*, page 107, West Palm Beach, FL: Learning Sciences International
5. Christodolou, D. (2016) *Making Good Progress? The Future of Assessment for Learning*, page 55, Oxford: Oxford University Press
6. Didau, D. (2015) *What if Everything You Knew About Education Was Wrong?* pages 277–290, Carmarthen, UK: Crown House
7. Ibid. page 277
8. Ibid. page 277
9. Ibid. pages 281–282
10. Wiliam, D. (2016) *Leadership [For] Teaching Learning: Creating a Culture Where All Teachers Improve so that All Students Succeed*, page 100, West Palm Beach, FL: Learning Sciences International
11. Christodolou, D. (2016) *Making Good Progress? The Future of Assessment for Learning*, page 170, Oxford: Oxford University Press
12. Ibid. pages163–179
13. Allison, S. and Tharby, A. (2015) *Making Every Lesson Count*, page 210, Carmarthen, UK: Crown House
14. Christodolou, D. (2016) *Making Good Progress? The Future of Assessment for Learning*, page 167, Oxford: Oxford University Press
15. Brown, P., Roediger III, H., and McDaniel, M. (2014) *Make it Stick: The Science of Successful Learning*, page 41, London: Harvard University Press
16. Endres, T. and Renkl, A. (2015) 'Mechanisms Behind the Testing Effect: An Empirical Investigation of Retrieval Practice in Meaningful Learning' in *Frontiers in Pscyhology*, Volume 6, page 3
17. Alexander, R. (2012) *Improving Oracy and Classroom Talk in English Schools: Achievements and Challenges*, pages 2 and 6, Cambridge: Cambridge University Press
18. Didau, D. (2014) *The Secret of Literacy*, page 73, Carmarthen, UK: Crown House
19. Christodolou, D. (2016) *Making Good Progress? The Future of Assessment for Learning*, page 47, Oxford: Oxford University Press
20. Rosenshine, B. (2012) 'Principles of Instruction: Research-Based Strategies That All Teachers Should Know' in *American Education*, spring 2012, page 14
21. Wiliam, D. (2016) *Leadership [For] Teaching Learning: Creating a Culture Where all Teachers Improve so that All Students Succeed*, page 110, West Palm Beach, FL: Learning Sciences International
22. Allison, S. and Tharby, A. (2015) *Making Every Lesson Count*, page 230, Carmarthen, UK: Crown House

23. Wiliam, D. (2016) *Leadership [For] Teaching Learning: Creating a Culture Where All Teachers Improve so that All Students Succeed*, page 101, West Palm Beach, FL: Learning Sciences International
24. Christodolou, D. (2016) *Making Good Progress? The Future of Assessment for Learning*, page 25, Oxford: Oxford University Press
25. Ibid. page 211
26. Ibid. page 157
27. Ibid. page 92
28. Koretz, D. (2008) *Measuring Up*, page 49, Cambridge, MA: Harvard University Press
29. Rosenshine, B. (2012) 'Principles of Instruction: Research-Based Strategies That All Teachers Should Know' in *American Education, spring 2012*, page 17
30. Entwistle, N. (2000) *Promoting Deep Learning Through Teaching and Assessment: Conceptual Frameworks and Educational Contexts*, page 8, a paper to be presented at the TLRP Conference, Leicester, November 2000
31. Willingham, D. (2009) *Why Don't Students Like School?*, page 100, San Francisco, CA: Jossey-Bass
32. Nuthall, G. (2005) 'The Cultural Myths and Realities of Classroom Teaching and Learning: A Personal Journey' in *Teachers College Record, Volume 107*, page 928
33. Endres, T. And Renkl, A. (2015) 'Mechanisms Behind the Testing Effect: An Empirical Investigation of Retrieval Practice in Meaningful Learning' in *Frontiers in Pscyhology, Volume 6*, page 2
34. Christodolou, D. (2016) *Making Good Progress? The Future of Assessment for Learning*, pages 113–137 and 193, Oxford: Oxford University Press
35. Ibid. page 125
36. Ibid. page 127
37. Ibid. page 184–188
38. Didau, D. and Rose, N. (2016) *What Every Teacher Needs to Know About . . . Psychology*, pages 89–91, Woodbridge, UK: John Catt
39. Ibid. page 93
40. Koretz, D. (2008) *Measuring Up*, pages 30–31, Cambridge, MA: Harvard University Press
41. Christodolou, D. (2016) *Making Good Progress? The Future of Assessment for Learning*, page 131, Oxford: Oxford University Press
42. Ibid. page 84
43. Ibid. page 139
44. Ibid. pages 79–111
45. Ibid. page 98
46. Ibid. page 129
47. Rosenshine, B. (2012) 'Principles of Instruction: Research-Based Strategies That All Teachers Should Know' in *American Education, spring 2012*, page 17
48. Lemov, D., Woolway, E. and Yezzi, K. (2012) *Practice Perfect: 42 Rules for Getting Better and Better*, San Francisco, CA: Jossey-Bass

49. McInerney, D., Wing-yi Cheng, R., Mo Ching Mok, M. and Kwok Hap Lam, A. (2012) 'Academic Self-Concept and Learning Strategies: Direction of Effect on Student Academic Achievement' in *Journal of Advanced Academics, Volume 23*, page 249, SAGE

Chapter 8

Testing to permanency

"Tests can be valuable learning events."[1]

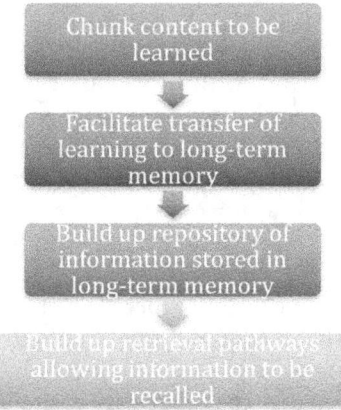

Why test?

How much do students get wrong because they don't know, and how much do they get wrong because they once knew but don't any more?

In *What Every Teacher Needs to Know About ... Psychology*, Didau and Rose point out that "the only way to see if something has been retained over time and transferred to a new context is to look at what students can do later and elsewhere."[2]

The 'testing' element of the instruction process is the 'newbie,' based on relatively recent (or relatively recent to teachers) developments in cognitive science. As Karpicke explains in *Retrieval-Based Learning*, there has been an emphasis on teaching strategies that encode knowledge rather than the use of retrieval cues to retrieve and reconstruct knowledge: "There seems to be a tacit assumption that successful encoding or construction of knowledge, in itself, is sufficient to ensure learning."[3] In comparison, he points out that retrieval should be seen "Not only as a tool for assessing learning but also a tool for enhancing learning."[4]

The learning process happens over time. For information to be 'learned' rather than 'learning,' it needs first to be stored in the long-term memory.

This occurs through extended deliberate practice. However, once stored in the long-term memory, learning also needs to be retrievable. Karpicke suggests that, "Learning is altered by the act of retrieval itself."[5] The more that knowledge is retrieved, the stronger and more durable learning becomes.

Long-term memory is crucial to learning. Daniel Willingham explains that, "your brain is set up to save you from having to think ... when we can get away with it, we don't think. Instead we rely on our memory."[6] Expert learners are those who have more domain specific knowledge stored in their long-term memory.

However, retrieval connections between long-term and working memory are also essential for effective recall. It's no good having something stored in the long-term memory if it is irretrievable. Some cognitive scientists have envisaged this as a 'long-term working memory,' which allows expert learners to keep information in long term memory directly accessible by means of effective retrieval cues in short-term memory.[7]

Robert Bjork explains[8] that there are two elements to memory strength:

- Storage strength: How securely knowledge has been learned; and
- Retrieval strength: How retrievable knowledge is.

Obviously, the aim of our teaching is to both ensure that knowledge is securely learned through deliberate practice, and to provide opportunities for students to strengthen their retrieval of knowledge.

How much do students get wrong because they don't know, and how much do they get wrong because they once knew but don't any more?

The process of retrieving information prevents forgetting from occurring. David Didau suggests that, "the best time to [retrieve information] ... is just at the moment we're about to forget."[9]

The testing effect

The 'testing effect' is the finding that long-term memory is increased when learning includes retrieval of the knowledge to be 'learned' through testing with proper feedback. Other common names for this process are:

- Retrieval practice;
- Practice testing; and
- Test-enhanced learning.

The act of retrieval that occurs during a test makes the knowledge tested more memorable. This 'testing effect:'

- Is greater than the effect of re-studying information without testing;
- Produces better retention of knowledge than mind-mapping;
- Increases as more tests are given; and
- Is linked to spacing, i.e. tests are more effective if they are spaced rather than massed.[10]

In their helpful guide into *What Works, What Doesn't*, Dunlosky *et al.* identified "two clear winners" [11] when it came to effective study practices. The first of these was self-testing. As they point out, "short, frequent exams are most effective, especially when test takers receive feedback on the correct answers. Practice testing works even when its format is different from that of the real test [and] the beneficial effects may last for months to years."[12] This reinforces Daisy Christodolou's point made in *Making Good Progress?* that students to not always need to practice in the "final form."[13]

Brown *et al.* therefore argue that we should "stop thinking of testing as a dipstick to measure learning,"[14] when in fact retrieving knowledge from long-term memory:

- Strengthens long-term memory;
- Strengthens retrieval pathways; and
- Interrupts the 'forgetting' process.

And – as we already know from our understanding of 'desirable difficulties' – the more difficult the retrieval, the stronger its benefit to learning.

Retrieval for learning

Roediger *et al.* outline the benefits of testing in their research paper: *Ten Benefits of Testing and Their Applications to Educational Practice*:[15]

1. The testing effect: Retrieval of knowledge aids its later retention by slowing down forgetting. The process of retrieving knowledge from long-term memory makes it easier to recall in the future and can eventually embed either propositional or procedural knowledge so that it becomes "reflexive."[16]
2. Testing identifies knowledge gaps. Roediger *et al.* point out that "students' knowledge of effective study strategies is quite poor without specific instruction."[17] Therefore they tend to choose less effective strategies such as re-studying and re-reading, which produce familiarity and therefore give a misleading illusion of fluency. In comparison, testing helps students to judge the real extent of their knowledge more accurately.
3. The occurrence of 'test-potentiated learning.' Roediger *et al.* explain that taking a test improves the amount of knowledge that students are able to acquire in subsequent study sessions.[18] 'Test-potentiated learning' appears to increase in effect with the number of tests, and when feedback is provided after tests.
4. Testing improves organisation of knowledge. Roediger *et al.* suggest that retrieval "causes students to organise information more than does reading."[19]
5. Testing improves knowledge transfer to new contexts. Roediger *et al.* found some evidence to suggest that "repeated testing improved far transfer:"[20] students' ability to transfer knowledge from one context to another.
6. The occurrence of a 'retrieval-induced facilitation effect:' Testing can facilitate the retrieval of knowledge that was not tested. Roediger *et al.* explain that testing can improve the retention of other knowledge that is related to that tested and integrated into the study process; however, conversely, a 'retrieval induced forgetting effect' can also occur when students 'forget' non-tested knowledge because of their focus on the knowledge to be tested.[21] A further explanation of retrieval-induced forgetting can be found at the Learning and Forgetting Lab website.[22]
7. Testing improves students' metacognitive monitoring of their learning by giving them more accurate information about this. By understanding what they actually know, and don't know,

students are able to make more efficient and effective study choices. Because it avoids the trap of familiarity, which can give the illusion of fluency, testing, unlike re-reading, prevents students from gaining false confidence and an unrealistic sense of how well they know material. Interestingly, research has found that, "testing reduced students' confidence even while aiding their performance," while repeated studying had the reverse effect.[23]

8. Testing prevents interference from prior information when learning new information. When sets of information are learned in succession over 'elongated' study sessions (such as linear GCSE or A Level courses), "proactive interference" can occur when the previous information learned hinders the retention of new information. Roediger *et al.* suggest that testing between these study episodes can reduce the impact of proactive interference.[24]

9. Testing provides formative feedback to teachers and students informing their future teaching and studying. Roediger *et al.* suggest that, "teachers often drastically overestimate what they believe their students to know." Therefore testing provides a useful reality check.[25]

10. Frequent testing forces students to develop more effective study habits. In particular addressing students' tendencies:
    i. To cram (or 'massed' study) before tests rather than spacing out their learning;
    ii. To under-learn information;
    iii. To focus on learning the 'wrong' information, for example not spending enough time on difficult information; and
    iv. To use ineffective learning strategies.[26]

Dunlosky *et al.* found that when testing was less regular, it was more likely to lead to cramming before a test, whereas daily testing led to study that was more effectively distributed over time.[27]

Caveat

The paean on the benefits of testing is not universal. In a review article published in 2015,[28] Gog and Sweller point out that the 'testing effect' "decreases as the complexity of learning materials increases;" therefore it may be used more effectively in learning the basic knowledge, that provides the building blocks for advanced understanding, than when learning complex information. This is because in the case of complex information:

- The benefits of testing in improving the organisation of knowledge (point 4 above) are no longer so obvious as the information is already "highly related"; and
- Restudy "may be more effective," because the overconfidence that students can gain from restudy of simple materials (outlined in point 7 above) is less likely to occur. Gog and Sweller ponder whether the 'testing effect' is therefore "not so much a consequence of beneficial processes occurring during testing, as it is of suboptimal processes during restudy."

Aspects of effective retrieval

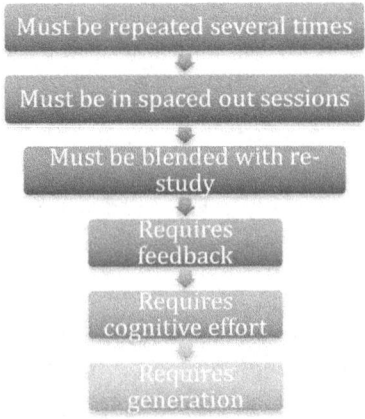

Effective retrieval must be repeated several times

In *When is Practice Testing Most Effective for Improving the Durability and Efficiency of Student Learning*, Rawson and Dunlosky found that, "increasing the number of practice tests leads to greater levels of performance on subsequent criterion measures."[29]

Effective retrieval must be in spaced out sessions

Brown *et al.* point out that, while massed studying or cramming can lead to higher performance in initial tests, it also leads to faster forgetting than retrieval practice that is spaced over time. This obviously makes cramming particularly ineffective for mock exams. In comparison, retrieval practice that is spaced over time, allowing forgetting to occur between tests, introduces a 'desirable difficulty' that results in more durable long-term retention.[30]

Similarly, Rawson and Dunlosky found that spacing out practice tests with increasing intervals between each test was more effective than a massed sequence of practice tests.[31]

Effective retrieval must be blended with re-study

Rawson and Dunlosky found that when practice tests were combined with re-studying, this was more effective than a programme of just testing or just re-studying.[32]

Effective retrieval requires feedback

Rawson and Dunlosky point out that the provision of corrective feedback in the form of either feedback or re-teaching is "particularly important" when students have made mistakes, in order to remove these errors and misconceptions.[33] Gog and Sweller emphasise the necessity of feedback, suggesting that "it is possible that feedback is often a prerequisite for finding a testing effect."[34]

Effective retrieval requires cognitive effort

Brown *et al.* explain that, "repetition by itself does not lead to good long-term memory."[35] Learning happens when we think hard; therefore, the more 'desirable difficulty' incorporated into the retrieval process, the greater the retentive effects.

In *Mechanisms Behind The Testing Effect*,[36] Endres and Renkl examine three theories for explaining the 'testing effect.'

The first, elaborative retrieval theory, suggests that testing strengthens existing retrieval cues and builds new ones. They point out that within this theory the 'desirable difficulty' of a challenging test leads to "higher invested mental effort" which therefore strengthens the learning.[37]

Effective retrieval requires generation

Brown *et al.* suggest that tests requiring students to generate an answer for themselves, rather than 'recognition' tests (multiple-choice questions, for example) "appear to be more effective."[38] Similarly, Endres and Renkl find that if unspecified-goal hypothesis (the third of the theories that they examine) explains the 'testing effect' then "learning is best if an open initial task (free recall) is used in the ... [practice] phase."[39]

Endres and Renkl suggest that if transfer appropriate processing theory (the second of the theories that they examine) explains the 'testing effect,' then "learning is best if the test tasks in the ... [practice] phase and in the assessment phase are of the same type."[40]

Endres and Renkl conclude that any tests used should "require learners to invest substantial mental effort."[41]

Other aspects of retrieval to consider

Collaborative recall

In their study into the benefits of collaborative recall,[42] Blumen and Stern point out that collaborative recall can benefit individual memory through:

- Re-exposure: When individuals recall information in a social context, they are often re-exposed to additional information that they would not have re-called alone; and
- Cross-cuing: The re-call of other group members can also cross-cue, or trigger recall of new information, not available to students if recalling alone.

Pre-testing

In their research on the pre-testing effect, Richland *et al.* explain that testing is as much a tool for acquiring knowledge as it is for measuring knowledge. They find that, counter-intuitively, sitting a test *before* the knowledge has been explained and learned, and when therefore 'failure' is inevitable:

- Increases learner attention; and
- Improves learning of the subsequently presented information.[43]

Therefore, they conclude that, "as long as the test material ... is followed by instruction that provides answers to the tested questions ... even if tests are not answered successfully, they have the potential to improve future learning."[44] Robert Bjork suggests that in pre-testing, multi choice questions may be more effective because they direct the students' attention "more broadly" during the follow-up study.[45]

Ten questions for the professional practitioner to ask

Table 8.1

Question	Action
1. How do I know what students get wrong because they don't know it, and what they get wrong because they don't know it anymore?	
2. How do I use testing in lessons?	
3. How do I plan testing in a spaced way over the medium-term curriculum sequence?	
4. How do I blend testing with re-study?	
5. How do I ensure that effective feedback is given after tests to correct errors?	
6. How do I use generative testing?	
7. How do I use collaborative recall?	
8. How do I use pre-testing?	
9. How do I use regular review in lessons?	
10. How do I ensure that students self-test?	

Ten ways to save time with testing to automaticity

Save future revision and recap time by:

1. Including a review of learning into every lesson, e.g. a question from last lesson, last week, last month and last year, so that knowledge is embedded into long-term memory as you go.
2. Teaching students how to memorise information in your subject so that they can do this efficiently and effectively.
3. Teaching parents how to help their children to memorise information in your subject.
4. Teaching knowledge only to initial correct recall then moving on in order to create time for spaced opportunities to recall information.

5. Ensuring that all your students (and parents) are familiar with the findings of Dunlosky *et al.* on effective learning strategies, and therefore, that they do not waste time on ineffective learning strategies like re-reading.
6. Using regular tests and quizzing to embed basic knowledge.
7. Setting regular tests and quizzing as homework and holiday homework to free up lesson time.
8. Not allowing students to cram for mock examinations, which will cause faster forgetting on the information.
9. Improving students' recall by setting up collaborative recall activities.
10. Using pre-testing to quicken future learning.

Where does retrieval fit in the instruction sequence?

Retrieval needs to be built into the instruction sequence.

In *Principles of Instruction*, Rosenshine argues that daily review is an essential element of teaching. He suggests that a 5–10 minute review at the start of lessons can strengthen connections between prior and new knowledge, building fluency and automaticity.[46]

Rawson and Dunlosky suggest a sequence in which new knowledge is practised only until it can be correctly retrieved during the initial learning session, and then returned to in future learning sessions. They find that, "In contrast to the limited benefit of a higher learning criterion [than one correct retrieval], the benefit of increasing the number of relearning sessions is substantial."[47] Their "tentative recommendation"[48] is that students participate in at least three relearning sessions, which can decrease in length as learning becomes more secure.

The introduction of retrieval into the instruction sequence obviously has profound consequences for planning of lessons and medium term curriculum sequences, in terms of both what we do and the order that we do it in. It involves:

- Building retrieval sessions into lessons – this is probably most effectively done when new knowledge is presented. The traditional time to 'start' new learning is at the start of a lesson, but, in order to take advantage of the opportunities presented by 'flipped learning' for students to build on initial explanation in the lesson as homework, this 'start' could be moved to another point in the lesson. In Chapter 4 of *Making Every*

Lesson Count, Allison and Tharby suggest a way of building retrieval quizzing into lessons that is time-saving, easy to introduce and therefore well worth using.[49]
- Changing curriculum sequences. In traditional curriculum sequencing, a sequence of topics are taught in 'massed' form with recap occurring (if there is time) at the end of the course. The findings of Rawson and Dunlosky suggest a spaced sequence (taking advantage of 'desirable difficulties') in which topics are taught more briefly: To initial correct recall, but then revisited more regularly throughout the course.
- Inserting testing into the instructional sequence at both the start of learning (pre-testing) and, subsequently, through the 'learning' to 'learned' process.

Notes

1. Richland, L., Kornell, N. and Kao, L. (2009) 'The Pre-Testing Effect: Do Unsuccessful Retrieval Attempts Enhance Learning?' in *Journal of Experimental Psychology: Applied, Volume 15*, page 254
2. Didau, D. and Rose, N. (2016) *What Every Teacher Needs To Know About . . . Psychology*, page 14, Woodbridge, UK: John Catt
3. Karpicke, J. (2012) 'Retrieval-Based Learning: Active Retrieval Promotes Meaningful Learning' in *Current Directions in Psychological Science, Volume 21*, page 158, SAGE
4. Ibid.
5. Ibid.
6. Willingham, D. (2009) *Why Don't Students Like School?*, pages 6 and 8, San Francisco, CA: Jossey-Bass
7. Ericsson, K. and Kintsch, W. (1995) 'Long-Term Working Memory' in *Psychology Review, Volume 102*, pages 211–245
8. https://bjorklab.psych.ucla.edu/research/
9. Didau, D. (2015) *What if Everything You Knew About Education Was Wrong?* page 223, Carmarthen, UK: Crown House
10. Roediger, H., Putnam, A. and Smith, M. (2011) 'Ten Benefits of Testing and Their Applications to Educational Practice' in *Psychology of Motivation and Learning, Volume 55*, pages 3, 7 and 29, Elsevier
11. Dunlosky, J., Rawson, K., Marsh, E., Mitchell, J. and Willingham, D. (2013) 'What Works, What Doesn't' in *Scientific American Mind, Volume 24*, page 48
12. Ibid. page 49
13. Christodolou, D. (2016) *Making Good Progress? The Future of Assessment for Learning*, page 23, Oxford: Oxford University Press
14. Brown, P., Roediger III, H., and McDaniel, M. (2014) *Make it Stick: The Science of Successful Learning*, page 19, London: Harvard University Press

15. Roediger, H., Putnam, A. and Smith, M. (2011) 'Ten Benefits of Testing and Their Applications to Educational Practice' in *Psychology of Motivation and Learning*, Volume 55, pages 1–36, Elsevier
16. Brown, P., Roediger III, H., and McDaniel, M. (2014) *Make it Stick: The Science of Successful Learning*, pages 28–29, London: Harvard University Press
17. Roediger, H., Putnam, A. and Smith, M. (2011) 'Ten Benefits of Testing and Their Applications to Educational Practice' in *Psychology of Motivation and Learning*, Volume 55, page 9, Elsevier
18. Ibid. page 10
19. Ibid. page 12
20. Ibid. page 16
21. Ibid. pages 18–19
22. https://bjorklab.psych.ucla.edu/research/#rif
23. Roediger, H., Putnam, A. and Smith, M. (2011) 'Ten Benefits of Testing and Their Applications to Educational Practice' in *Psychology of Motivation and Learning*, Volume 55, pages 20–21, Elsevier
24. Ibid. page 22
25. Ibid. page 24
26. Ibid. page 27
27. Dunlosky, J., Rawson, K., Marsh, E., Nathan, M., and Willingham, D. (2013) 'Improving Students' Learning with Effective Learning Techniques: Promising Directions from Cognitive and Educational Psychology' in *Psychological Sciences in the Public Interest*, Volume 14(1), page 39, SAGE publishing
28. Gog, T. and Sweller, J. (2015) 'Not New, But Nearly Forgotten: The Testing Effect Decreases or Even Disappears as the Complexity of Learning Materials Increases' in *Educational Psychology Review*, Volume 27, pages 247–264, Springer
29. Rawson, K. and Dunlosky, J. (2012) 'When is Practice Testing Most Effective for Improving the Durability and Efficiency of Student Learning?' in *Education Psychology Review*, Volume 24, page 421, Springer
30. Brown, P., Roediger III, H., and McDaniel, M. (2014) *Make it Stick: The Science of Successful Learning*, page 31, London: Harvard University Press
31. Rawson, K. and Dunlosky, J. (2012) 'When is Practice Testing Most Effective for Improving the Durability and Efficiency of Student Learning?' in *Education Psychology Review*, Volume 24, page 421, Springer
32. Ibid. page 420
33. Ibid. page 420
34. Gog, T. and Sweller, J. (2015) 'Not New, But Nearly Forgotten: The Testing Effect Decreases or Even Disappears as the Complexity of Learning Materials Increases' in *Educational Psychology Review*, Volume 27, pages 247–264, Springer
35. Brown, P., Roediger III, H., and McDaniel, M. (2014) *Make it Stick: The Science of Successful Learning*, page 14, London: Harvard University Press

36. Endres, T. and Renkl, A. (2015) 'Mechanisms Behind the Testing Effect: An Empirical Investigation of Retrieval Practice in Meaningful Learning' in *Frontiers in Pscyhology*, *Volume 6*, pages 1–6
37. Ibid. page 2
38. Brown, P., Roediger III, H., and McDaniel, M. (2014) *Make it Stick: The Science of Successful Learning*, page 41, London: Harvard University Press
39. Endres, T. and Renkl, A. (2015) 'Mechanisms Behind the Testing Effect: An Empirical Investigation of Retrieval Practice in Meaningful Learning' in *Frontiers in Pscyhology*, *Volume 6*, page 3
40. Ibid. page 2
41. Ibid. page 5
42. Blumen, H. and Stern, Y. (2011) 'Short-Term and Long-Term Collaboration Benefits on Individual Recall in Younger and Older Adults' in *Memory & Cognition*, *Volume 39(1)*, pages 147–154, Springer
43. Richland, L., Kornell, N. and Kao, L. (2009) 'The Pre-Testing Effect: Do Unsuccessful Retrieval Attempts Enhance Learning?' in *Journal of Experimental Psychology: Applied*, *Volume 15*, pages 243–244
44. Ibid. page 252 and 254
45. https://bjorklab.psych.ucla.edu/research/
46. Rosenshine, B. (2012) 'Principles of Instruction: Research-Based Strategies That All Teachers Should Know' in *American Education*, *spring 2012*, page 13
47. Rawson, K. and Dunlosky, J. (2012) 'When is Practice Testing Most Effective for Improving the Durability and Efficiency of Student Learning?' in *Education Psychology Review*, *Volume 24*, page 425–427, Springer
48. Ibid. page 431
49. Allison, S. and Tharby, A. (2015) *Making Every Lesson Count*, page 137, Carmarthen, UK: Crown House

Chapter 9

Marking for improvement

An 'open loop' control system that does not use feedback to check that its output has achieved the desired goal of its input cannot control its errors.

Traditionally in teaching, marking was a retrospective action that took place separately to teaching and planning. First we planned our schemes of work in folders that lived on our shelves next to our department handbooks. Then we delivered our lessons. Then we marked our students' books retrospectively and in line with our marking policies that work be marked every week/fortnight/term/year/decade, sprinkling them with comments like 'good work, keep it up' or inevitably rhetorical questions such as 'where is your underlining?' And it would be true to say that marking has never been the favourite activity of most teachers. More recently, the focus has been on formative feedback and dialogue with students, leading to the bête noire of 'triple marking.'

The importance of marking that is both effective, but also efficient and manageable for teachers, is considerable. In 2014, marking was identified as the single biggest contributor to unsustainable workload in the Department for Education's Workload Challenge consulta-tion.[1] The Education Endowment Foundation review into the evidence on written marking that followed this in 2016 suggested that "teachers should consider marking less, but marking better."[2]

I want to consider the word 'mark' as another 'Ronseal' word. When we 'mark' something, we 'notice or pay careful attention to' it (OED definition). Another definition of 'marking' that is worth considering is to 'make a visible impression on' (OED definition). Our 'marking' could therefore be considered as anything that we, or our students, do that pays careful attention to work and makes a visible impression (improvement) to it.

There are arguably three reasons to mark work:

1. To provide feedback to the teacher on the effectiveness of instruction. It is this feedback that allows teaching to be a 'responsive' activity rather than merely a 'delivery' activity.
2. To provide feedback to the student on how to improve their performance.
3. To value the work. We will not receive work from students that is "strong and accurate and beautiful"[3] unless we, and our students, pay careful attention to it. It is for this last reason that most students like their work to be 'marked' even when they cannot read, or do not understand, the feedback that they have received.

The challenge therefore is how to find ways of paying careful attention to students' work that are manageable for teachers.

What are the features of effective marking?

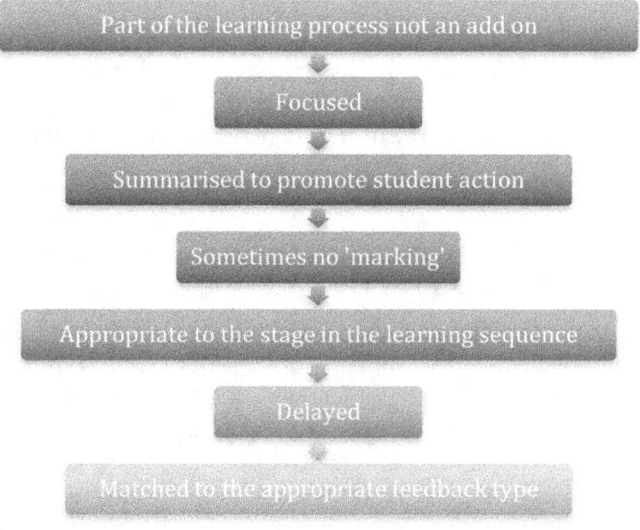

Effective marking occurs as part of the learning process, not as an add on

For the first two criteria above to be met, marking must be part of the instruction process. This means that the traditional separation of planning, teaching and retrospective marking will not be sufficient because it does not allow for 'responsive' teaching. Marking should be interwoven with instruction, as well as informing planning. In *Feedback in Written Instruction*, Kulhavy explained that when feedback and review are combined, "the process itself takes on the forms of new instruction, rather than informing the student solely about correction."[4]

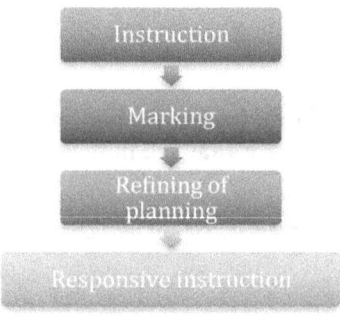

This does not mean that marking has to be a lengthy process in which student work is taken in and laboriously proof read. The 'marking' that occurs in the initial stages of instruction for example, may be the live 'marking' of a hinge question asked in the lesson to ascertain levels of understanding.

Effective marking is focused

Traditionally, lengthy and time-consuming marking has been seen as a sign of dedicated teaching; however, with the right type of marking, less is more, in terms of effectiveness as well as manageability. Remember that we are teachers not copy editors.

Feedback to students should focus on one or two improvement strategies: Simple, logical steps that students need to master before moving on. In their 2007 analysis of feedback and review of the evidence related to effective feedback, *The Power of Feedback*, Hattie and Timperley point out that specific goals about how to do a task more effectively are "more effective . . . because they focus students' attention."[5] Similarly, the Education Endowment Foundation's review of the evidence on written marking found that "specificity of feedback is a key determinant of its impact on performance."[6]

In *Embedded Formative Assessment*, Dylan Wiliam criticises the type of accurate and descriptive, but non-diagnostic feedback that prevents the learner improving: "The teacher had written, 'You need to be more systematic in planning your scientific inquiries.' I asked the student what that meant to him, and he said, I don't know. If I knew how to be more systematic, I would have been more systematic the first time.'"[7]

Effective marking is summarised to promote student action

Traditionally, marking has corrected mistakes for students, however in this process it is the teacher rather than the student who is thinking hard about the work. It makes no sense, and does not promote effective student learning, for teachers to spend more time on a student's work than the student has.

Summarised marking encourages students to think hard and re-engage with their own work in a corrective process, thereby promoting effective learning. Once again, less is more in terms of effectiveness and manageability. In their excellent chapter on marking, Shaun Allison and Andy Tharby provide examples of symbol marking.[8]

Similarly, a process in which teachers write comments for students to read does not lead to students thinking hard. Less time consuming for the teacher, and more thought provoking for the student, is a process in which the teacher gives 'live' verbal feedback and the students write targets and comments on their work.

The Education Endowment Foundation's review of evidence on written marking found evidence that mistakes and errors should also be marked differently.

- Mistakes should be marked wrong but not corrected so that students have to correct the work for themselves and therefore think about their mistakes. This process of 'thinking hard' will make it less likely that students will repeat their mistakes.

- Errors should be corrected by feedback, as the students do not have the knowledge to work out how to correct the errors for themselves.[9] Correction of errors is delivered more quickly and powerfully by 'live' re-teaching and re-explanation to an individual, group or class, rather than by lengthy and repeated written comments.

Effective marking is sometimes no 'marking'

It is sometimes forgotten that feedback is not automatically effective but depends on the context. In the wrong circumstances, feedback can actually lead to less effective learning. Hattie and Timperley point out that where students lack sufficient knowledge, further teaching is "more powerful"[10] than feedback; therefore if the learning demonstrates less than 80 per cent success, the teacher is far better re-teaching the information that has not been sufficiently mastered.

This prevents:

- The teacher spending disheartening time producing lengthy written feedback that;
  - Disheartens the students; and
  - Results in less effective learning than had a quicker process of re-teaching been adopted because the learning gap to be closed is, at this stage, too wide for feedback to be effective.

Students also need to be trained out of 'recognition' marking. It is important that students' work is noticed and valued, but there are quicker and more efficient ways of doing this verbally, or through rewards structures, than 'recognition' marking of pages of work that do not require teacher feedback.

Effective marking is appropriate to the stage in the learning sequence

Just as a lesson is not a unit of learning, an individual piece of work is not necessarily a unit of learning. For this reason marking sequences can take place over series' of work:

Table 9.1

Task	Type of Marking	Rationale
Task acquisition	Live marking	During task acquisition, live marking allows the teacher to immediately correct any errors and misconceptions that students have acquired before these become embedded in their schemas.
First process work	Guided student marking	Guided student marking *before submission to the teacher* builds students' self-regulation strategies and encourages them to 'think hard' about the work; therefore ensuring that the work submitted for teacher marking is more rewarding for both teacher and students.
Second process work	Teacher marking	At this stage students can submit a piece of work that has been informed by guided student marking and the subsequent re-drafting, giving the teacher a sense of students' learning.

Using a sequence like the one above across two or three pieces of work prevents the time-consuming sequence of a single piece of work being submitted, re-drafted and re-submitted, which might not always be possible due to curriculum time constraints. It also encourages students to see the deep structure of process work (like essay writing) by applying feedback from one example of the process to another.

It is also worth building student proof reading or error checking into the marking sequence so that:

- Students are encouraged to build effective self-regulatory habits;
- Students need to think hard about their work;
- Students are encouraged to produce work of 'excellence';
- Teacher marking time is saved because accidental errors are corrected;
- The teacher is encouraged by the higher performance ensuing from initial proof reading or error checking; and
- The teacher can focus on actual errors and misconceptions in their feedback.

Guided student marking can occur once students have completed a piece of work and involves them self-marking their work as a 'noticing' and correcting activity. It should be:

- Closely guided by the teacher;
- Focused on the common errors and misconceptions that students might have made;
- Quantitative rather than qualitative; and
- Specific.

It is often effectively done against a checklist.

Examples might include students checking how many times they have referenced the question in their answer, or counting the number of pieces of evidence that they have cited, or checking for simple grammatical or procedural mistakes. This process of structured checking and correcting of work builds student self-regulation and reduces the time that the teacher then needs to spend in error correction.

Hattie and Timperley explain that where students have effective error detection skills this can be "very powerful."[11] Therefore the marking sequence would look as follows:

Table 9.2

Task	Type of Marking	Rationale
Task acquisition	Live marking	During task acquisition, live marking allows the teacher to immediately correct any errors and misconceptions that students have acquired before these become embedded in their schemas.
Student correction of errors	Student self-regulation	Ensures that students 'think hard' about, and correct, initial errors and conceptions.
First process work	Guided student marking	Guided student marking builds students' self-regulation strategies and encourages them to 'think hard' about the work; therefore ensuring that the work submitted for teacher marking is more rewarding for both teacher and students.
Student proof reading	Student self-regulation	The teacher guides students in proof checking for errors and misconceptions that the teacher anticipates using pedagogical content knowledge. This process is then used to inform the production of the second piece of process work.
Second process work	Teacher marking	At this stage students can submit a piece of work that has been informed by guided student marking and the subsequent re-drafting, giving the teacher a sense of students' learning.
Student correction of errors	Student self-regulation	Ensures that students 'think hard' about and correct errors and conceptions remaining at this stage.

In their chapter on feedback, Allison and Tharby describe a process of "gritty editing."[12] The Education Endowment Foundation's review of the evidence on written marking concluded that time should be set aside for students to engage with written feedback in order to "maximise . . . the impact"[13] of teacher marking.

Effective marking may be delayed

As explained below, depending on the stage of learning, feedback should either be immediate or delayed. In the initial stages of learning, immediate corrective feedback is important. In the later stages of learning however, delayed feedback becomes a 'desirable difficulty.' In *What if Everything You Knew About Education Was Wrong?* David Didau points out the undesirability of students becoming "crazed feedback junkies"[14] who are over-dependent on teacher feedback.

Effective marking is matched to the appropriate feedback type for this stage of the learning

Hattie and Timperley identify three types of effective feedback:

- Task (FT);
- Process (FP); and
- Self-Regulation (FR).

In comparison, they warn against feedback on 'self' (FS) that is insufficiently related to feedback on the task or process.[15]

Task feedback

This type of feedback occurs in the second stage of the assessment process outlined in Chapter 7 (assessment of task fluency), in which students are acquiring new knowledge at task rather than process level. At this stage of learning, **immediate** correction of errors is important in order to prevent students embedding incorrect information into their schemas that could be hard to unpick. It also helps to speed up the learning process because students do not waste time on misconceptions or errors.

The most manageable type of teacher feedback at this stage is therefore 'live' marking in the classroom, in which the teacher circulates during the lesson. This allows the teacher to respond in 'real time' to student understanding or lack of understanding. The 'five minute flick' of work also allows understanding to be assessed at this stage.

Live marking should be ***brief***. In *Principles of Instruction*, Rosenshine found that the optimum time for student-teacher contact was 30 seconds or less.[16]

Hattie and Timperley suggest that this feedback should:

- Be simple rather than complex; and
- Move students from task to process understanding.[17]

In *Making Good Progress?* Daisy Christodolou suggests that feedback at this task level can be more effectively diagnostic and formative because the activity is not yet over-complex.[18]

Process feedback

This type of feedback fits into the third and fourth stages of the assessment process outlined in Chapter 7 (assessment of process fluency and of deep structure fluency) because it involves feedback about the deeper processes or structures underlying tasks. Hattie and Timperley point out that feedback at this level is necessary for students to gain deep understanding.[19]

At this stage of learning, **delayed** feedback is more helpful as "immediate error correction during fluency building can detract from the learning of automaticity."[20]

While it is important for students to interact critically with their work using guided marking practices, teacher marking is also necessary to provide feedback to the teacher on the effectiveness of instruction. In *Leadership [For] Teacher Learning*, Dylan Wiliam refers to this as "retroactive regulation of learning"[21] in which the teacher reflects on teaching after this has occurred.

Teacher marking time outside lessons is probably most effectively spent on FP feedback that develops the processes underlying tasks and is therefore transferrable to unseen versions of the process. In comparison, the Education Endowment Foundation's review of the evidence on written feedback found "some evidence"[22] that teachers focus on literacy when marking rather than giving process feedback.

Self-regulated feedback

This type of feedback fits across the stages of the assessment process outlined in Chapter 7. Hattie and Timperley suggest that the "most effective" feedback develops learning on a spectrum from task understanding through process understanding to self-regulation, in which the student is able to "create internal feedback and to self-assess."[23] In their study on feedback interventions, Kluger and

DeNisi suggest that the use of self-regulated feedback could "yield impressive gains in performance."[24]

Self and peer assessment are only effective when students are able to make secure, critical (and teacher reviewed) judgements about work. For this reason they are best guided by worked examples and models of excellence and based on quantitative or simple, rather than qualitative or complex judgements. Hattie and Timperley point out that 'cues' like worked examples and models of excellence work because, "feedback is more effective when it provides information on correct rather than incorrect responses."[25]

Taxonomies of error can also be used as part of guided student marking or teacher feedback. These can either be created:

- In advance based on the teacher's pedagogical content knowledge and used to prevent misconceptions and errors as a piece of pre-feedback, or to guide student checking of work.
- As a result of teacher marking of work, responding to actual student errors and misconceptions. The creation of a single taxonomy of errors sheet is quicker to produce than twenty to thirty individual comments on work. It is also more durable as a 'permanent' piece of feedback that can be used on future work as a piece of pre-feedback

Using critique

In *An Ethic of Excellence*, Ron Berger circumvents the pitfalls of shallow, uninformed self and peer assessment by using critique sessions to develop students' self-regulatory skills.

He suggests the use of three types of critique:

- Gallery critique in which the work of all students is displayed;
- In-depth critique in which a single piece of work is critiqued using the appropriate academic register; and
- Guest critique from an expert.[26]

As Berger points out, unless students are explicitly taught the skill of critique, this process is not "particularly useful."[27] In *Making Every Lesson Count*, Allison and Tharby suggest that where students are able to compare their work to better examples, the feedback that they therefore receive is "potentially richer, quicker and more detailed . . . than a written comment."[28] In addition, feedback from models has the advantage that it can be 'seen' and therefore lacks the abstract element of written feedback.

Using verbal feedback

It is worth remembering that verbal feedback can be more powerful than written feedback because of its direct and emphatic nature. It is also quicker to give and means that feedback can be given to groups of students rather than one individual response at a time. In *Making Every Lesson Count*, Allison and Tharby point out that, "it is far easier to be detailed and personalised when feeding back personally."[29]

Reducing feedback

It is the complaint of many teachers that they have to write the same piece of feedback again and again as students repeatedly fail to take on board the advice that they have been given.

As Daisy Christodolou points out in *Making Good Progress?*, students "know what they are supposed to do, yet they don't do it reliably."[30] Christodolou argues that deliberate practice helps to reduce this 'knowing–doing' gap. One way of developing this deliberate practice and ensuring that students do what they are supposed to do is to use pre-marking checklists, based on previous feedback, which students complete before submitting work. It saves even more time if the students construct these checklists themselves using the feedback that they have been given. It is also worth teachers considering tracking the feedback that they have given so that they are able to train students into the habit of:

This is far more effective than a timewasting process in which the teacher writes the same ineffective target again and again over repeated pieces of work.

To grade or not to grade?

The Education Endowment Foundation's review of the evidence on written marking, *A Marked Improvement?*, found evidence that grading has a positive impact on girls, probably because they tend to underestimate their performance, and a negative impact on boys and low-attaining students, probably because they are more likely to overestimate their performance.[31] They found that the hypothesis that students concentrate on grades rather than formative feedback "is supported by the majority of studies."[32] This is reinforced by Daisy Christodolou's argument in Chapter 7, that grading systems are not sufficiently sensitive to provide reliable formative feedback.[33] Therefore it might be more effective to give feedback based on the proportion of correct learning, with 80–90 per cent as a threshold, than to give grades.

Ten questions for the professional practitioner to ask

Table 9.3

Question	Action
1. How do I use feedback to inform my teaching?	
2. How do I use feedback to improve the performance of students?	
3. How do I show that I value students' work?	
4. How do I ensure that marking is an integral part of the instruction process, not an 'add on' after the event?	
5. How do I ensure that my feedback is specific and understandable?	
6. How do I make students 'think hard' about my feedback?	
7. How do I differentiate between errors and mistakes?	
8. How do I mark differently across the learning stages?	
9. How do I use Task Feedback, Process Feedback and Self-Regulation Feedback?	
10. How do I use critique?	

Twenty ways to save time with marking for improvement

1. Save time by using 'live' verbal rather than written feedback in the initial stage of learning.
2. Save time by writing shorter comments focused on 1–2 improvement strategies.
3. Save time by modelling first to increase student clarity and reduce misconceptions.
4. Save time by using summarised marking.
5. Save time by replacing teacher writing of comments with teacher verbal feedback and students writing comments and targets.
6. Reduce teacher marking by students correcting mistakes.
7. Reduce teacher marking by re-teaching errors.
8. Reduce teacher marking by marking over sequences of work rather than 'teacher marking' every piece of work.
9. Save time by not 'recognition' marking.
10. Save time in teacher marking by using guided student marking as pre-feedback that tackles misconceptions and reduces the amount of teacher marking.
11. Deepen student 'thinking hard' and learning opportunities by planning student correction and self-regulation activities.
12. Save time by delaying feedback on the later stages of learning.
13. Save time by making reviews brief: A 30 second 'live' interaction or '5 minute flick' through books.
14. Focus written teacher marking on process feedback (FP).
15. Save time by getting students to provide self-regulated feedback based on models.
16. Save time by producing a single taxonomy of errors rather than writing a class set of comments.
17. Save time by replacing written feedback with emphatic verbal feedback.
18. Save time by students completing a pre-marking checklist to reduce mistakes ...
19. ... And ensure that students produce this checklist based on previous feedback, rather than the teacher.
20. Save time by reducing the use of grades.

For the teacher looking to develop effective feedback strategies I would also recommend the chapter on this in *Making Every Lesson Count*.[34]

Where does marking fit in the instruction cycle?

Table 9.4

Assessment	Examples of this type of assessment	Manageable feedback
Of initial understanding	Hinge questions Written or oral	Immediate, 'live' verbal feedback.
Of task fluency	Short practice questions Written or oral	'Live' marking in the lesson.
Of process fluency	Long practice questions Written	Interspersing of guided student marking and teacher marking over a series of tasks.
Of deep structure	Interleaved process questions Written	
Of permanent learning	Regular, spaced, generative retrieval quizzes	Students create and mark self-quizzes. **However, Rawson and Dunlosky point out that the provision of corrective feedback in the form of either feedback or re-teaching is "particularly important" when students have made mistakes on tests in order to remove these errors and misconceptions.**[1]
Of synoptic learning	Interleaved questions	
All types	Spaced teacher marking	

1 Rawson, K. and Dunlosky, J. (2012) 'When is Practice Testing Most Effective for Improving the Durability and Efficiency of Student Learning?' in *Education Psychology Review*, Volume 24, page 420, Springer

Notes

1. www.gov.uk/government/publications/workload-challenge-analysis-of-teacher-responses
2. Elliot, V., Baird, J., Hopfenbeck, T., Ingram, J., Thompson, I., Usher, N., Zantout, M., Richardson, J., and Coleman, R. (2016) *A Marked Improvement? A Review of the Evidence on Written Marking*, page 12, University of Oxford, Education Endowment Foundation
3. Berger, R. (2003) *An Ethic of Excellence*, page 1, Portsmouth, NH: Heinemann
4. Kulhavy, R. (1977) 'Feedback in Written Instruction' in *Review of Educational Research, Volume 47*, page 212
5. Hattie, J. and Timperley, H. (2007) 'The Power of Feedback' in *Review of Educational Research, Volume 77*, page 87, American Research Association and SAGE
6. Elliot, V., Baird, J., Hopfenbeck, T., Ingram, J., Thompson, I., Usher, N., Zantout, M., Richardson, J., and Coleman, R. (2016) *A Marked Improvement? A Review of the Evidence on Written Marking*, page 20, University of Oxford, Education Endowment Foundation
7. Wiliam, D. (2011) *Embedded Formative Assessment*, page 120, Indiana, IN: Solution Tree Press
8. Allison, S. and Tharby, A. (2015) *Making Every Lesson Count*, pages 175–176, Carmarthen, UK: Crown House
9. Elliot, V., Baird, J., Hopfenbeck, T., Ingram, J., Thompson, I., Usher, N., Zantout, M., Richardson, J., and Coleman, R. (2016) *A Marked Improvement? A Review of the Evidence on Written Marking*, page 12, University of Oxford, Education Endowment Foundation
10. Hattie, J. and Timperley, H. (2007) 'The Power of Feedback' in *Review of Educational Research, Volume 77*, page 91, American Research Association and SAGE
11. Ibid. page 86
12. Allison, S. and Tharby, A. (2015) *Making Every Lesson Count*, pages 173–174, Carmarthen, UK: Crown House
13. Elliot, V., Baird, J., Hopfenbeck, T., Ingram, J., Thompson, I., Usher, N., Zantout, M., Richardson, J., and Coleman, R. (2016) *A Marked Improvement? A Review of the Evidence on Written Marking*, page 16, University of Oxford, Education Endowment Foundation
14. Didau, D. (2015) *What if Everything You Knew About Education Was Wrong?* page 254, Carmarthen, UK: Crown House
15. Hattie, J. and Timperley, H. (2007) 'The Power of Feedback' in *Review of Educational Research, Volume 77*, pages 96–97, American Research Association and SAGE
16. Rosenshine, B. (2012) 'Principles of Instruction: Research-Based Strategies That All Teachers Should Know' in *American Education, spring 2012*, page 19
17. Hattie, J. and Timperley, H. (2007) 'The Power of Feedback' in *Review of Educational Research, Volume 77*, pages 91–92, American Research Association and SAGE
18. Christodolou, D. (2016) *Making Good Progress? The Future of Assessment for Learning*, page 90, Oxford: Oxford University Press

19. Hattie, J. and Timperley, H. (2007) 'The Power of Feedback' in *Review of Educational Research*, *Volume 77*, page 93, American Research Association and SAGE
20. Ibid. page 98
21. Wiliam, D. (2016) *Leadership [For] Teaching Learning: Creating a Culture Where All Teachers Improve so that All Students Succeed*, page 110, West Palm Beach, FL: Learning Sciences International
22. Elliot, V., Baird, J., Hopfenbeck, T., Ingram, J., Thompson, I., Usher, N., Zantout, M., Richardson, J., and Coleman, R. (2016) *A Marked Improvement? A Review of the Evidence on Written Marking*, page 14, University of Oxford, Education Endowment Foundation
23. Hattie, J. and Timperley, H. (2007) 'The Power of Feedback' in *Review of Educational Research*, *Volume 77*, page 94, American Research Association and SAGE
24. Kluger, A. and DeNisi, A. (1996) 'The Effects of Feedback Interventions on Performance: A Historical Review, a Meta-Analysis, and a Preliminary Feedback Intervention Theory' in *Psychological Bulletin*, *Volume 119*, page 278
25. Hattie, J. and Timperley, H. (2007) 'The Power of Feedback' in *Review of Educational Research*, *Volume 77*, page 85, American Research Association and SAGE
26. Berger, R. (2003) *An Ethic of Excellence*, pages 94 and 96, Portsmouth, NH: Heinemann
27. Ibid. page 94
28. Allison, S. and Tharby, A. (2015) *Making Every Lesson Count*, page 114, Carmarthen, UK: Crown House
29. Ibid. page 182
30. Christodolou, D. (2016) *Making Good Progress? The Future of Assessment for Learning*, page 49, Oxford: Oxford University Press
31. Elliot, V., Baird, J., Hopfenbeck, T., Ingram, J., Thompson, I., Usher, N., Zantout, M., Richardson, J., and Coleman, R. (2016) *A Marked Improvement? A Review of the Evidence on Written Marking*, page 10, University of Oxford, Education Endowment Foundation
32. Ibid.
33. Christodolou, D. (2016) *Making Good Progress? The Future of Assessment for Learning*, page 193, Oxford: Oxford University Press
34. Allison, S. and Tharby, A. (2015) *Making Every Lesson Count*, pages 165–200, Carmarthen, UK: Crown House

Planning for effective instruction Part 2

Designing effective curriculum sequences

This section of the book is intended to supplement the section on effective planning to be found at the end of Chapter 3, and to reinforce the sections explaining where an element of the teaching process fits within the instruction sequence to be found at the end of Chapters 4 to 9.

At the end of Chapter 3, I suggested that:

- An individual lesson is not the unit of learning;
- Instructional sequences are fluid and interconnected; and
- The text book should be reconsidered.

This section of the book considers the effective construction of medium-term curriculum sequences, particularly those designed to promote the 'learning' to 'learned' process.

In, *War Against Schools: Academic Child Abuse*, Siegfried Engelmann argues that "instructional sequences have the capacity to make students smart or not ... When the curriculum fails, the teaching will fail."[1]

1. Planning curriculum sequences using core and threshold knowledge

In Chapter 2, I referred to **threshold concepts** as a distinct category within the 'core concepts' that form the building blocks of understanding.

In *An Introduction to Threshold Concepts*, Glynis Cousin describes these as "central to the mastery of their subject."[2] She suggests that focusing on threshold concepts allows teachers to make "refined decisions" about what to teach: "A 'less is more' approach to curriculum design."[3]

Understanding of a threshold concept may take time to acquire, and the knowledge within it may be 'troublesome' for students to reconcile with their existing schemas; nevertheless, understanding threshold concepts is necessary in order for the learner's under-standing to progress because threshold concepts are generally:

- Transformative;
- Irreversible; and
- Integrative.

The importance of threshold concepts to deep and permanent learning, which moves beyond shallow knowledge and "mimicry" of understanding, means that they need to feature prominently in learning and curriculum sequences, and Meyer and Land therefore suggest that they have "significant pedagogical importance."[4]

How should this understanding inform our planning of curriculum sequences?

Step 1. Identify the core *and* threshold concepts that make up your subject's curriculum.

Plan curriculum sequences around threshold concepts as the "jewels in the curriculum."[5]

Step 2. Assess students' understanding against these threshold concepts.

Cousins explains that this requires us to "gaze backwards"[6] because, as teachers, we should have made irreversible progress through our subject's threshold concepts and therefore think like experts rather than novices.

Capture the journey through threshold concepts in your subject. What are the common misconceptions? What are the best routes through the threshold concepts?

> Step 3. Permit liminal spaces.
>
> Cousins suggests that teachers must "hold their students through liminal states."[7] This involves allowing and encouraging confusion in order for students to be prepared to abandon mimicry and shallow understanding.
>
> Step 4. Plan repeated learning over time.
>
> Cousin writes that, "Mastery of a threshold concept often involves messy journeys back and forth and across conceptual terrain." This means that curriculum planning needs to allow revisiting and looping back.

Table 10.1

Topic	Core Knowledge	Threshold Concepts	'Liminal' learning activities	Common misconceptions to be assessed	Revisiting opportunities: One Two Three
___	___	___	___	___	___
___	___	___	___	___	___
___	___	___	___	___	___
___	___	___	___	___	___

2. Planning curriculum sequences that opitimise cognitive load theory

In Chapter 6, I referred to Cognitive Load Theory. This can inform the planning of activities across the curriculum sequence.

Table 10.2

Learning Phase	Activity	Cognitive rationale	Assessment and feedback
Early	Gaining basic understanding of the domain through explanation of models and worked examples.	This frees the learner from performance demands so that they can concentrate on gaining understanding.	Immediate 'live' assessment (through hinge questions) and feedback is most useful at this stage to prevent misconceptions becoming embedded.
Intermediate	Focusing on how to solve problems through worked examples and self-explanation.	Active self-explaining is important in this phase to learn the rationale of how to apply basic knowledge	Increasingly delayed feedback as students gain expertise.
Late	Developing speed and accuracy through problem solving.	The aim in this phase is automaticity, therefore self-explanations are not helpful and worked examples are redundant.	

Renkl and Atkinson[8]

3. Planning for permanent learning

A frequent mistake that is made in medium-term planning is to focus too much on content delivery and therefore to allow too little time for practice relevant to the stage of learning, retrieval, and opportunities for feedback and review. It is important that all of the elements of instruction outlined in Chapters 4 to 9 are built into the instruction sequence in an intertwined and fluid manner:

- Modelling and explanation;
- Extensive deliberate practice through the stages of learning;
- Accurate assessment through the stages of learning including regular testing; and
- Feedback and review for improvement.

In line with the above, in his excellent blog, *Pragmatic Education*, Joe Kirby examines Siegfried Engelmann's 'Direct Instruction' approach to teaching and characterises its features as:

- Precise example sequences;
- High-pace questioning of up to 10 learner responses per minute;
- Continuous instant feedback;
- Extended practice drills with no more than 15 per cent of the lesson spent on new content; and
- Rapid correction of misconceptions.[9]

Considerations when creating time in planning medium term curriculum sequences:

- How can homework and 'flipped learning' be used to create more time?
- How should learning be spaced across a course:
  i. Less time spent on 'massed' practice of topics and more time spent on 'spaced' practice.
  ii. Less time spent on revision topics and more time spent on regular retrieval throughout the course.

More details of this type of curriculum sequencing can be found at the end of Chapter 8.

- How does planning ensure that the activities that take place in lesson time are those in which the role of the teacher is essential and that more independent student work is done pre- and post lesson in order to create more lesson time.

4. Planning across the stages of learning

In Chapter 7, I referred to the stages of learning:

- Initial understanding;
- Task fluency;
- Process fluency;
- Deep structure fluency;
- Permanent learning; and
- Synoptic learning.

It is important that these stages are built into medium term planning.

Ten questions for the professional practitioner to ask

Table 10.3

Questions	Action
1. Does my medium-term planning differentiate between core and threshold concepts?	
2. Does my medium-term planning build in 'liminal' learning activities?	
3. Does my medium-term planning allow sufficient revisiting and looping back in the teaching of threshold concepts?	
4. Does my medium-term planning incorporate Cognitive Load Theory?	
5. Does my medium-term planning give appropriate amounts of time to each of the elements of instruction?	
6. Does my medium-term planning incorporate elements of 'Direct Instruction'?	
7. Does my medium-term planning make optimal use of 'flipped learning'?	
8. Does my medium-term planning reduce the amount of 'massed' practice and increase the amount of 'spaced' practice?	
9. How much retrieval time is built into my medium-term planning?	
10. Does my medium-term planning take into account the stages of learning?	

Ten ways to save time with planning

1. In an overstuffed curriculum, save time by focusing teaching on threshold concepts.
2. Save time by incorporating the principles of Cognitive Load Theory into medium-term planning . . .
3. . . . Both in terms of the stage of learning (early, intermediate or late) . . .
4. . . . And the novice or expertise status of the learners based on their prior knowledge.
5. Save instruction time by considering use of Engelmann's methods of Direct Instruction.

6. Save lesson time by using homework and 'flipped learning' effectively.
7. Save revision time at the end of courses by building retrieval practice into medium-term planning.
8. Save time on 'massed' practice to increase time for 'spaced' practice.
9. Save teacher time by considering which elements of instruction require direct teacher input, and which don't ...
10. ... Then make more use of structured pre- and post lesson learning activities.

Notes

1. Engelmann, S. (1992) *War Against Schools: Academic Child Abuse*, page 7, Portland, OR: Halcyon House
2. Cousin, G. (2006) 'An Introduction to Threshold Concepts' in *Planet, Volume 17*, page 4
3. Ibid.
4. Meyer, J. and Land, R. (2003) 'Threshold Concepts and Troublesome Knowledge: Linkages to Ways of Thinking and Practising Within the Disciplines' in *Improving Student Learning – Ten Years On*, C. Rust (Ed), page 7, Oxford: OCSLD
5. Cousin, G. (2006) 'An Introduction to Threshold Concepts' in *Planet, Volume 17*, page 5
6. Ibid.
7. Ibid.
8. Renkl, A. and Atkinson, R. (2003) 'Structuring the Transition From Example Study to Problem Solving in Cognitive Skill Acquisition: A Cognitive Load Perspective' in *Educational Psychologist, Volume 38*, pages 15–22, Lawrence Erlbaum Associates
9. https://pragmaticreform.wordpress.com/2013/02/02/direct-instruction/

Index

abstraction 108
'accessible challenge' 36–37
accuracy 129
'active learning' 37
'activity learning' 49
'add ons' 73
Against the Odds: Disadvantaged Students Who Succeed in School (OECD) 64
Alexander, R. 4, 6, 7, 12, 24, 122
Allison, S.: on academic language 81; on excellence 61; on feedback 160–161; on 'good practice' 3; on learning objectives 69; on learning process 55; on marking 153, 157; on modelling 62–63, 71, 73; on practice 98; on principles of instruction 52; on questioning 119, 121–122, 124; on repetition 110; on responsive explanation 85; on retrieval 147
ambitiousness 67
Aristotle 26
assessment: key features of effective 129–130; stages of 124–128
Assessment of Learning 123
Atkinson, R. 82, 104
atomisation of instruction 2–3
automaticity 104, 105, 107–108, 145–146

background knowledge 82, 83–84
Bad Science (Goldacre) 8

Barber, M. 19
Bartle, K. 6
Becoming a High Expectation Teacher (Rubie-Davies) 68–69
behaviour management 53
Berger, R. 30, 62, 66–67, 68, 70, 160
Biesta, G. 3, 14, 23, 50
Bjork, R. 12, 42, 138, 145
Bloom's Taxonomy 100
Blue Peter 70
Blumen, H. 144
Bower 87
Brain Gym 8
Brian Simon and Pedagogy (Alexander) 7
Brown, P.: on assessment 122; on automaticity 107; cognitive science and 12; on encoding 87, 88; on interleaving 109; on learning process 35, 41, 42, 55–56, 63, 83; on memory 38; on practice 96, 98, 99; on problem solving 104–105; on self-explanation 87; on testing 139, 142–144

Caroll 64
Carpenter, S. 111
Carter Review of Initial Teacher Training 12
Christodolou, D.: on assessment 120, 121, 122, 123, 125–126, 128, 129–130; on "deliberate

practice method" 98; on feedback 159, 161, 162; on generic skills approach 26, 29, 100–101; on schemas 108; on testing 139; on Wiliam 56–57
chunking 80, 82, 90
classroom climate 53
classroom management 53, 60
Class Teaching (Allison) 52, 69
closed questions 121–122, 129
Coe, R. 3, 10, 34, 35
"cognitive apprenticeship" 61, 102–103
cognitive effort 143
cognitive load 82, 88, 105, 113
Cognitive Load Theory 39, 105–106, 169–170
'cognitive short cuts' 90
collaborative recall 144
comparative judgement assessing 128
computer game theory 36
concreteness 80–81
content validity 129
"cookbook approach" 3
core knowledge 100, 167–169
Could Do Better (Oates) 29
counter-intuitiveness 41
Cousin, G. 167–169
cramming 141, 142–143
credibility 81–82
Critical Thinking (Willingham) 100
critique, using 160–161
cross-cuing 144
Cruddas, L. 24
cues, encoding and creating 87–88, 90, 138
curiosity 80
curriculum sequences 55, 167–171

deep structure 108–109, 127
delayed feedback 159
deliberate practice 98–99
'deliverology' 19
'delivery' model 56
DeNisi, A. 159–160
"deprofessionalising" of teachers 4, 24–25, 26

'desirable difficulties' 42–43, 109, 110, 139, 143, 147, 158
Didau, D.: on academic language 81; on 'activity learning' 49; on assessment 120, 129, 137; on automaticity 107; on 'desirable difficulties' 110; on encoding 88; on expectations 70; on explanation 81, 82; on far transfer 101; on feedback 13; on 'fun' over learning 35; on knowledge 36; on knowledge transfer 105; on learning misconceptions 43; on learning objectives 60, 61; on lesson observations 10; on memory 38, 39–40; on 'meta beliefs' 7; on misconceptions 84; on modelling 63, 71; on retrieval 138; on schemas 62; on "short-cut culture" 22; on success 102; on teacher talk 78; on teaching English 68; on teaching profession 5, 9, 23, 41; on threshold concepts 56; on verbal assessment 122; on working memory 88
differentiation 74
difficulty model of assessment 129
'Direct Instruction' approach 171
'distributed practice' 110
Do Learners Really Know Best? (Kirschner and Merrienboer) 7–8
domain-specific knowledge 81–82, 101
Domain Specific Knowledge (Tricot and Sweller) 81, 108
Do We Know a Successful Teacher When We See One? (Strong et al.) 10
drilling 107–108
drill versus scrimmage 99
Dunford, J. 21–22, 24–25
Dunlosky, J. 20, 38, 86–87, 110, 139, 141, 142, 143, 146, 147

easiness 37, 43
Education, Education, Education project 12

Education Endowment Foundation 11, 21, 150, 153, 157, 159, 162
Education and Neuroscience (Howard-Jones) 8
Education Policy Institute 19
effective instruction: planning for 55–59; principles of 49–53
effective learning, principles of 34–45
effective teaching: confusion over 2–10; 'looks' of 10
elaborative interrogation 86
elaborative retrieval theory 143
Embedded Formative Assessment (Wiliam) 153
Emile (Rousseau) 7
emotions 82
Endres, T. 122, 128, 143, 144
Engelmann, S. 97, 167, 171
Entwistle, N. 126
Ericsson, K. 97
errors 153–154
An Ethic of Excellence (Berger) 30, 62, 66–67, 160
evidence-based teaching 11–15
Evidence into Practice (Rose) 38, 87
excellence: de-constructing 70–71; description of 67–71; reasons for 66–67
expectations 68–70
expertise reversal effect 104–105, 106
experts, novices versus 102–103, 108
Explaining for Understanding 51, 52, 77–92
explanation, elements of 83–89
extraneous load 105

'fading' practice 103, 112
familiarity 81, 83
'far transfer' 101, 140
feedback: delayed 159; effective retrieval and 143; formative 141; process 159; reducing 161; self-regulated 159–160; task 158–159; types of 158–160; verbal 161

Feedback in Written Instruction (Kulhavy) 152
Final Report of the Commission on Assessment without Levels 14–15
financial incentives 21
Fisher, C. 20
fluency 64–66, 70, 95–96, 112–113, 125–127
Fordham, M. 29
formative assessment 119–121
formative feedback 141
formative practice and assessment 37–38
free recall testing 122
Fullan, M. 2, 5, 11, 13, 23, 25, 51

generation, effective retrieval and 143–144
germane load 105
Gladwell, M. 97
Gog, T. 141–142, 143
Goldacre, B. 8
"gritty editing" 157
guided practice 102

Hargreaves, D. 2, 5, 11, 13, 23, 25, 50, 51
Hart, S. 69
Hattie, J. 11, 12–13, 19, 152–153, 154, 156, 158, 159, 160
Heath, C. 79, 80, 81, 82
Heath, D. 79, 80, 81, 82, 95
Hempenstall, K. 9
The Hidden Lives of Learners (Nuthall) 40, 127
Hirsch, E. D. 100
Howard-Jones, P. 8
Husbands, C. 34

illusion of fluency 119, 128
Improving Education (Coe) 3, 10, 34
Improving Students' Learning with Effective Learning Techniques (Dunlosky et al.) 20, 38, 86–87
inclusiveness 68–69
Increasing Pupil Motivation 21

individualisation 6–7
individual lessons 55–56
initial understanding 124–125
instruction, elements of 51–52
instructional sequences: assessment in 133; explanation in 83–89, 91–92; interconnected 56–57; marking and 164; practice in 113–114; retrieval and 146–147
interleaving 109
Interleaving Helps Students Distinguish among Similar Concepts (Rohrer) 109
intervention-loaded teaching 19–22
intrinsic load 105
An Introduction to Threshold Concepts (Cousin) 167–168

James, M. 34

Karpicke, J. 137–138
Kidd, D. 72
Kirby, J. 171
Kirschner, P. 7–8, 39, 78–79, 103
Kluger, A. 159–160
'knowing–doing' gap 161
knowledge: background 82, 83–84; core 100, 167–169; domain-specific 81–82, 101; hidden body of 125; organisation of 140, 142; pedagogical content 27–29; 'powerful' 27, 28–29, 35–36, 80, 108; practice and 99–101; primary 36; procedural 38, 68, 99, 140; propositional 38, 68, 99, 140; 'rehearsal' of 96; secondary 36; specialised 27; subject 28–29; 'troublesome' 43–44
knowledge base for teachers 26
Knowledge and the Future School (Young and Lambert) 25, 27, 28, 35–36, 68, 77–78
Knowledge and Teaching (Shulman) 26, 49, 50
Koretz, D. 126, 129
Kulhavy, R. 152

labelling from assessment 130–131
'lag effect' 111
Lambert, D. 25, 27, 28, 29, 35–36, 68, 80
Land, R. 41, 43–44, 168
Leadership [for] Teacher Learning (Wiliam) 13, 121, 159
learning, relationship between pedagogy and 34–45
Learning and Forgetting Lab 12, 42, 140
learning objectives 60, 61, 69
learning what we think about 37–38
Learning Without Limits (Hart) 69
Lemov, D. 63, 97–98, 99, 102, 108, 131
Leonard, G. 35, 99
lesson planning 55–59, 167–173
lesson types, fetishising 3–6
liminality 43
long-term memory 38–41, 42, 77, 138–139

Maggs, A. 9
Make it Stick (Brown) 12, 35, 38, 41, 55–56, 83, 87, 96, 98, 99, 105, 107, 109
Making Every Lesson Count (Allison and Tharby) 3, 52, 61, 62, 85, 98, 110, 119, 125, 146–147, 160–161, 163
Making Good Progress (Christodolou) 56–57, 98, 100–101, 120, 121, 128, 130, 139, 159, 161
A Marked Improvement? (Education Endowment Foundation) 162
marking: appropriate 154–157; delayed 158; description of 150; features of effective 151–160; feedback type and 158–160; focused 152–153; reasons for 151; summarised 153–154
Marking for Improvement 51, 52, 150–164
Mastery (Leonard) 35, 99
mastery curve 99

McDaniel, M. 12
McInerney, D. 131
Measuring Up (Koretz) 129
Mechanisms Behind the Testing Effect (Endres and Renkl) 143
memory 37, 38–41, 42, 138
Merrienboer, J. van 7–8
'meta beliefs' 7
Meyer, J. 41, 43–44, 168
misconceptions: common 43; elimination of 84
mistakes 43, 63, 106, 153
Modelling of Excellence 51, 52, 60–74
Model of School Learning 64
motivation 102
Mount, Ferdinand 101
multiple-choice questions 122

National College of School Leadership 23
National Curriculum 29
National Strategies 1–2, 6
novices versus experts 102–103, 108
Nuthall, G. 40, 56, 86, 109, 127

Oates, T. 6–7, 29, 57–58, 70
Ofsted, fetishising lesson types and 3–6
'open loop' control system 150
open questions 121–122
oracy 91
Outliers (Gladwell) 97

Peal, R. 3–4
Pearce, J. 34
pedagogical content knowledge 27–29
pedagogical underpinning, lack of 6–9
pedagogy, definition of 1
Pedagogy into Practice 1–3, 6, 22–23, 56
peer assessment 123, 160
Perfect Practice (Lemov) 63
performance improvement, addiction of 36
permanent learning 127, 170–171

Personalised Learning – a Practical Guide 7
Playing the Game (Peal) 4
Plowden Report 7
Pollard, A. 34
'powerful knowledge' 27, 28–29, 35–36, 80, 108
powerful pedagogy, description of 19–30
The Power of Feedback (Hattie and Timperley) 152
practice: about 95–97; aspects of 97–104; types of 107–111
Practice Perfect (Lemov et al.) 98, 102, 131
practice testing 139
Practising to Fluency 51, 52, 95–114
Pragmatic Education (Kirby) 171
precision 129
predictive validity 129
Preparing for a Renaissance in Assessment (Barber) 19
pre-testing 144–145
primary knowledge 36
Principles of Instruction (Rosenshine) 61, 63, 71, 73, 84–85, 101, 102, 124, 126, 146, 158
problem solving 104–105
procedural knowledge 38, 68, 99, 140
process feedback 159
process fluency 126
Professional Capital (Hargreaves and Fullan) 5, 23, 25, 50–51
proficiency, as term 66
progress checking 119
Project on Learning (Nuthall) 109
Promoting Deep Learning through Teaching and Assessment (Entwistle) 126
propositional knowledge 38, 68, 99, 140

quality model of assessment 129
quality over quantity 68
Questioning as Assessment 51, 52, 118–133

questions: to ask of learning 118–123; 'hinge' 124; multiple-choice 122; open and closed 121–122, 129; for professional practitioner to ask 45, 58, 72, 89, 111–112, 132, 145, 162, 172

Rawson, K. 142, 143, 146, 147
'recognition' marking 154
'recognition' testing 122
reducing feedback 161
re-exposure 144
Reflecting English (Tharby) 52
'rehearsal' of knowledge 96
reliability 129
Renkl, A. 82, 104, 122, 128, 143, 144
repetition 98, 142
research-based teaching 11–15
researchEd 11
responsive explanation 84–85
responsiveness 56–57, 62
'responsive teaching' 56–57
re-study 143
retained understanding 86–87
retention 21–22
retrieval: for learning 140–145; practice for 109–111
Retrieval-Based Learning 137–138
retrieval-induced facilitation effect 140
retrieval practice 139
retrieval strength 138
review, daily 146
Richland, L. 144–145
Robinson, M. 101
Roediger, H., III 12, 140–141
Rohrer, D. 109
Rose, N.: on assessment 129, 137; on 'desirable difficulties' 110; on encoding 87–88; on explanation 81, 82; on far transfer 101; on knowledge 36; on knowledge transfer 105; on memory 38, 39; on misconceptions 84; on schemas 62; on success 102; on teaching profession 9; on working memory 88

Rosenshine, B.: on assessment 124, 126; on domain knowledge 101; on explanation 84–85, 90; on misconceptions 84; on mistakes 63; on modelling 61, 62, 71, 73; on practice 96–97, 102; on review 146; on student–teacher contact 158; on success 101–102, 130
rote learning 107
Rousseau, J. -J. 7
Rubie-Davies, R. 68–69

scaffolding work 102–103
schemas 39, 62, 79, 90, 108
The School Leadership Journey (Dunford) 21–22, 24–25
secondary knowledge 36
The Secret of Literacy (Didau) 22, 57, 68, 71, 78, 122
seeing the point 60–63
self-assessment 123, 160
self-explanation 86–87
self-regulated feedback 159–160
self-testing 139
Seven Myths about Education (Christodolou) 26, 29
Shulman, L. 5, 9, 10, 15, 26–27, 28, 49, 77–78
Simon, B. 1, 6, 7, 9, 27, 34–35
simplicity 79–80
skills: higher versus lower 99–100; stages of acquisition for 104, 106; as term 66
spacing 110–111, 147
'spacing effect' 110–111
specialised knowledge 27
stages of learning 171
Stern, Y. 144
'sticky' explanations 79–83
Still No Pedagogy (Alexander) 6, 24
storage strength 138
Strong, M. 10
student explanation 86
student marking 156
study habits 141
subject knowledge 28–29
success 101–102, 113, 130–131

summarised marking 153
summative assessment 120, 122, 128
Sutton Trust 2, 11, 22, 34, 50
Sweller, J. 39, 81, 108, 141–142, 143
symbol marking 153
synoptic learning 128

task feedback 158–159
task fluency 125–126
teacher talk 78–79, 85, 90
Teacher Workload and Professional Development in England's Secondary Schools (EPI) 19, 21
Teaching: Notes from the Front Line (Kidd) 72
Teaching Adolescents to Become Learners 36, 87
Teaching and Learning Toolkit 11
Teaching as a Research-Based Profession (Hargreaves) 50
Teaching that Sticks (Heath and Heath) 79
Teaching Training Agency Annual Lecture 11
Teach Like a Champion (Lemov) 97–98
test-enhanced learning 139
testing: benefits of 140–142; effect of 139; reasons for 137–138; *see also* assessment
Testing to Permanency 51, 52, 137–147
test-potentiated learning 120, 140
textbooks, reconsidering 57–58
Tharby, A.: on academic language 81; on explanation 61; on feedback 160–161; on 'good practice' 3; on learning process 55; on marking 153, 157; on modelling 62–63, 71, 73; on practice 98; on principles of instruction 52; on questioning 119, 121–122, 124; on repetition 110; on responsive explanation 85; on retrieval 147

Theo, J. 9
thinking, use of versus learning 63–64
thinking aloud 62
thinking hard 35–37, 64, 95–96
Those Who Understand (Shulman) 26
threshold concepts 43–44, 56, 61, 84, 167–168
time allocation 20
time saving methods 59, 72–74, 90–91, 112–113, 132–133, 145–146, 163, 172–173
Timperley, H. 152–153, 154, 156, 158, 159, 160
Tomsett, J. 20
transfer appropriate processing theory 144
transformability 69
transposition, explanation as 84
Tricot, A. 39, 81, 108
Trivium (Robinson) 101
"troublesome knowledge" 43–44

unspecified-goal hypothesis 144

verbal assessment 122–123
verbal feedback 161
Visible Learning (Hattie) 11, 12

War Against Schools: Academic Child Abuse (Engelmann) 97, 167
What Every Teacher Needs to Know About . . . Psychology (Didau and Rose) 9, 36, 38, 88, 129, 137
What If Everything You Knew About Education Was Wrong? (Didau) 5, 7, 9, 10, 13, 23, 41, 49, 60, 78, 88, 120
What Makes Great Pedagogy? (Husbands and Pearce) 9, 23, 34, 55
What Makes Great Teaching? (Sutton Trust) 2, 11, 22, 28, 34, 50, 51
What Works Best in Education (Hattie) 12

What Works, What Doesn't (Dunlosky *et al.*) 110–111, 139
When is Practice Testing Most Effective for Improving the Durability and Efficiency of Student Learning (Rawson and Dunlosky) 142
White, R. 9
Why Don't Students Like School (Willingham) 12, 37, 127
Why Minimal Guidance During Instruction Does Not Work (Kirschner *et al.*) 8–9, 39, 78–79, 103
Why No Pedagogy in England? (Simon) 1, 9
Why Textbooks Count (Oates) 6–7, 57–58, 70
Why "What Works" Won't Work (Biesta) 3, 14, 23, 50
Wiliam, D.: on assessment 23, 56–57, 120, 121, 124, 125, 153; on automaticity 105; on experts and novices 102; on "retroactive regulation of learning" 159; on teaching profession 13, 14
Willingham, D.: on automaticity 107; on background knowledge 82, 83; on cognition 102; cognitive science and 12; on critical thinking 100; on deep structure 108, 127; on encoding 88; on explanation 80; on familiarity 81; on memory 37, 38, 73, 138; on 'meta beliefs' 7; on practice 96, 98
"wisdom of practice" 15, 50
Wooden, J. 108
'worked example effect' 103, 104
working memory 38–39, 73, 82, 88, 98, 103, 105–106, 112
workload 19, 21, 150
A World-Class Teaching Profession (Dept. of Education) 12, 49–50

Young, M. 25, 27, 28, 29, 35–36, 37, 68, 80

For Product Safety Concerns and Information please contact our EU representative GPSR@taylorandfrancis.com
Taylor & Francis Verlag GmbH, Kaufingerstraße 24, 80331 München, Germany

www.ingramcontent.com/pod-product-compliance
Lightning Source LLC
Chambersburg PA
CBHW052022290426
44112CB00014B/2342